**Ste**

# HEALIN



## About the Book

**HEALING STUDIES** is at once the fascinating record of how an average young decorator/painter turned healer and medium and it offers the interested readers a practical step-by-step guideline in how to develop their own psychic and sensitive faculties and what the foundation of spiritual healing actually is. The book is an inspiring read for everyone who wonders if the spirit world, spirit guides and spiritual healing are "real". It is written in an everyday language of a young man who used to be mostly interested in making a living, attractive girls and hanging out in a pub with his mates. No mumble-jumble of metaphysical or "holy" thinking, no pretence of enlightenment or the like but plain hands-on practical help for suffering people.

## About the Author Steven Levett: Spiritual Healer – Trance Healer - Medium

Steven started out life in South London as a painter and decorator. He initially experienced a few psychic events which amazed him, but Steven never really thought much of them, until he started to learn more about spiritual healing and mediumship. He trained at the Arthur Findlay College, Stansted and also with personal tutors until one day he met the renowned and internationally acclaimed master medium, spiritual teacher, researcher and author Gordon Smith and his then partner, Jim MacManus. Under their tutelage Steven developed his intuitive healing in a very sound and no-nonsense manner, discovering how much genuine compassion, humility, trust in spirit guidance and the spirit world are the main ingredients of effective spiritual healing. He has grown to be one of the most promising young spiritual healers in Europe who in a humble way shares his gifts. Gordon Smith has encouraged his probably best-known student to step up into the public eye and offer workshops and courses on his own. Gordon, as a bestselling author himself, helped Steven to pen these notes on his development, his spiritual practice and his courses.
*www.thespirituallifegroup.com*

**Table of Content**

## FOREWORD

I first encountered Steven Levett some years ago when he approached me at the end of one of my book-signings. My very first impression of Steven was that he was quite shy, down-to-earth and grounded, yet with a real desire to advance his spiritual knowledge.
Over the years which followed he sat in my home development circle where I was fortunate enough to watch him grow in his spiritual work as a healer and spiritual tutor, but more important was how he has grown as a man and become a close friend.

It is always good to see someone you have encouraged to fulfil their ambitions and achieve their goals in life, but when such goals involve helping others as Steven's have, then I do believe the word that comes to my mind to describe his gift of Spiritual Healing would be '*compassion.*'

Steven has always shown great patience during his own development; he was always happy to be taught slowly and correctly and this comes through in the way he now also teaches others who follow his own path to unfold and understand their spiritual gifts.

It really pleases me to see this young man grow and expand, sharing his knowledge with new students, keeping his feet on the ground and his trust well and truly in the spirit.
I feel he makes the development sound easy and clear and I am certain that those who read this book will find a great value, which they can add to their own search on the path of spiritual awakening.

Best Wishes,
Gordon Smith

# 1.

# AWAKE

When I was growing up with my parents and two sisters in South London, I honestly thought my life was as ordinary as the next person's. When I was quite young, I had a couple of funny, sort of psychic experiences and maybe the odd vivid dreams where I saw something happen that I couldn't have known about before it actually did. But all in all, it was more about playing football in the park with my mates which eventually progressed to sitting telling stories in the local pub with the same lads as I got older, usually discussing girls or football, or both on occasion.

Yes, nothing appeared to be too different as I said, that was until I turned twenty-one. I was working as a painter and decorator at the time and the only thing I could say I knew about the future was that I would be out with my mates down the pub come the weekend. Then one morning, very early I had a strange dream. It was strange because of how "real" everything appeared and how the very exaggerated quality of the characters and sounds of their voices was so graphic that it seemed to burn into my mind when I woke up. The images and sounds stayed with me for a whole day maybe even two.

In this dream, I can remember I was going to meet a girl and walk home with her and she was telling me something personal about one of my close mates called Jay. At the same moment when she began to speak, a flock of birds appeared to burst into the sky above our heads and right at that very same moment a piece of stone fell from the wall behind her and landed between us and a bus went past with my friend Jay on it which made the girl then shout. "Look, there's Jay on the bus, how weird!"

Though none of these events are in any way shocking to anyone, it wasn't until two months later I actually did meet this girl very randomly whilst walking home

from work she began talking to me and when her conversation turned to Jay and she began to get personal, then out of nowhere a flock of pigeons burst into the sky above us then the whole dream was back with me again. I then knew to expect the next two things in sequence, first the stone fell down and my head naturally turned to the road as the girl called out exactly as she had in the dream about Jay being on the passing bus.

I really didn't know what to make of that because at the time there wasn't anyone I could ask about this kind of stuff. As I said, I know that somewhere in the back of my mind I had had a few strange experiences when I was a kid, but nothing was ever made of it and I honestly tried to remember them later, but at this point they seemed so distant. I had a strange urge after that dream came to pass, I wanted to try and see if I could make predictions happen. It would be interesting to try and predict something for my mum or maybe one of my sisters I thought because they might be into that sort of thing and it might be a bit of a laugh. I honestly think I really wanted to see if my dream was just a dream that happened to me or was it because of something in me that the dream happened?

I remember sitting in my bedroom and thinking that I should concentrate on my mum and try to find things out about her life, or maybe her future ... I wasn't sure but I kind of got a feeling or something and then it didn't feel like a premonition or prediction about the future, but I could sense someone was beside me and I knew in a way that it was my nan, my mum's mother. As I was sensing this presence, I had a vision in my mind that my mum was standing in her bedroom looking at her own mother's wedding ring; this was followed by a complete urge that was so insistent that I went to my mum and told her what I was seeing. I truly had no idea why I was following this intuition but I was and when I went to tell my mum it came out like this. "Mum, I had a sense that my nan was with me, she wants you to know that she saw you take out her wedding ring last night." To say that my mum was astonished was an understatement; she was bloody gobsmacked. After a bit of humming and hawing and me explaining about my psychic dream and now this attempt to see if I could produce some psychic experience, she mellowed enough to explain that only the night before she was very drawn to take her mother's wedding ring out of the jewellery box and hold it in her hand as she stared for a while and went through some of her memories.

That was it for me, I wanted to find out more about these psychic and spiritual phenomena and once I found I could produce similar things for my two sisters, they also encouraged me to look for ways to develop my abilities and find out what was going on with me. I had no idea of the road which lay ahead for me, but now when I look back at that time, I can see that all of my early experiences where just my intuition being reawakened from the sleep it had gone into when I was just a child. So many mediums, psychics, healers and intuitives have very similar stories from their young lives, when episodes happen in order to bring their attention to the true natural gifts which they have within them.

It is so hard to understand that something which feels so different is sitting inside you and is just waiting to come out and though you know that it is not a thing that anyone else around you understands, not your close family or your friends, yet you know that it has to be allowed to grow. Not to allow your natural abilities to come to the fore would be such a shame.  I now know that it would leave you feeling like half a person, or like a lost soul wandering around the world with nowhere to belong. I believe that it was at this very moment in my young life that I realised my world was changing, though into what I did not know.  From being a very ordinary painter who went down the local pub with my mates and talking about football and girls, my existence couldn't have changed more if I'd walked into someone else's life.

## 2.

## FIRST STEPS

*"Everyone has some healing abilities within them, not everyone uses them on others."*

It was coming to the end of 2007 and I was sitting in front of fifty odd students in Frankfurt poised to give a talk about spiritual development. I say poised, but I was actually terrified to the point of melting into a pool of my own nervous sweat. I should have been reassured that my teacher, Gordon Smith, a renowned medium and spiritual teacher, was by my side but somehow that made me feel worse as it felt like I had two hurdles to get over. It would be the first time I would talk to students of spiritual development about what I had learned from my teacher and I would be confronting the dreaded fear I had of talking in public in front of someone who made it look so easy.

"How did I get here?" I sort of whispered to myself under my very dry breath, which made my mouth feel like it was coated with sandpaper. How *did* I actually get here? It was the strangest couple of years leading up to this moment. I had probably less than five minutes till I was due to stand up and address the people and instead of preparing what I should say my mind decided to think about how I arrived at this point in my life.

Since my endeavour to try to get psychic messages for my mother and sisters and since my predictive dream I had undertaken a course in trying to advance what I now realised was a natural psychic ability which had led me in some cases from the sublime to the ridiculous. Not long after my early attempts at intuitive readings on my family I was introduced to a friend of my sister, a woman called Annette, who was a psychic reader and my sister thought she might be able to give me some guidance. This guidance came in the form of two readings, which did help to explain things that had been happening to me. Annette was able to tell me about the experience I had with my nan without having any prior knowledge of what had happened and this impressed me, in fact it made me trust her and more than that, it made me think that truly something different was actually happening to me.

It was Annette who gave me CDs on proper meditation and she told me to use them and try to learn to calm my mind so that I could try to get clearer pictures of what was coming to me. She also told me that I should write down any strange dream or premonition so that I would have records of time and events to refer to if things came to pass. She was the first psychic I had met and she didn't appear too out of the ordinary. If anything, she was alright and very helpful, but there was more to what was happening to me than she could grasp I felt.

Now, maybe it's just the way I think but I couldn't help question everything after a while. I wondered if I had made it all up or if people were just telling me that what I said was right because they wanted to please me and with this kind of thinking I wanted to investigate further and look for someone with more knowledge than Annette. I wanted to find out more about the spirit world and why I should feel the presence of my nan and how I was able to say something to my mum that had really happened. So, either I was telepathic or a spirit person honestly gave me information, or was it all coincidence?

"This old life is funny at times." I kept saying that to myself as a habit but none more so than when I was about to throw in the towel and just give up on my search for spiritual answers. Because some months after my meeting with my sister's friend I had hit a wall. Nothing much was happening to me on a psychic level and I was feeling kind of let down. Part of me wanted there to be an afterlife where people like my nan could come and interact with me – there was a sort of comfort in that thought. I also felt that if there was a spirit world that they had opened something up in me and now it seemed they were not communicating at all. That was that, I thought if nothing comes to guide me to where to go next, I was going to give the whole thing a miss. Then low and behold out of nowhere my mum came walking into my bedroom with a copy of a newspaper she found in her pigeonhole in the supermarket where she collected her weekly magazines, it was the *Psychic News*. “The psychic what?” I said to her.

I was puzzled and quite astonished that there was a newspaper that reported on the world of psychics and mediums and all things about the spirit world. “Well, I never.” This was what I had been waiting for, it felt like a sign of some kind, it was an answer of sorts to the ultimatum I had thrown out to this unseen world. This small paper reported on events from spiritualist churches all across the UK and it gave details about mediums and events held by these people. I felt like Harry Potter just being introduced to a magical world or something. More magical though, was how it came to be put into my mum’s pigeonhole between her usual magazines!

The bottom line was, two things came of finding that paper. The first thing was I saw an advert about a medium and spiritual teacher who lived not too far from me who gave private tuition to mediums who were starting out. I thought this was for me, but after only a couple of visits to his home I quickly realised it wasn't. It was the second option that had much more of an effect on me, The Arthur Findlay College in Stansted, Essex.

This was a proper college where people could go to learn about the spirit world and how to develop mediumship and all things psychic. "This is the one for me." I said to my empty bedroom. It was a beautiful stately manor in the middle of the Essex countryside, not more than an hour from where I lived; Hogwarts on my doorstep so to speak. I made a call and in no time, I was booked on to a weeklong course in "Developing Mediumship".

My mind was too busy on the way to the Arthur Findlay College thinking about how it would feel to meet lots of people who were actual mediums and healers and trying to perceive what they would look like. Not to mention the many other students like me who would be going to find things out. My eyes were stunned at the magnificent building that was looming up in front of me when my taxi drew close to the building. At first, I was sort of in awe at the sight of the huge house and then my nerves kicked in and I wanted to tell the driver to turn back and take me to the train station. Suddenly I was reminded that I would have to talk to people and introduce myself and maybe even share some experiences which brought me to this place to find answers. But there was no going back now. I was there and something strong inside me made me remain as I went through with the signing in procedure and even though everyone around me seemed normal, I still had dread and great doubt in the pit of my stomach. I don't think I said anything more than *yeah*, or *nah*, to people who addressed me or asked me questions for the first full day; partly because I had never been in a building this grand and my eyes constantly scanned my surroundings and partly because I felt totally out of my depth.

I really don't remember much about the first day in the College, but I did relax a bit as the week went on and I went into my class which was held in one of the large sitting rooms and was taken by a medium called Sandy Baker. She was a bright happy looking woman in her forties and she made me relax as she spoke quite normally about the world of spirits, actually to her it seemed to be a matter of fact and nothing that special.

Sandy put me at ease and even when she took the group through meditation practices, I was able to let go a bit and it felt like the connection I had previously was starting to build again. I watched a demonstration of mediumship where Sandy and a man called Glyn Edwards gave messages from the spirit world to an audience in the room they call the sanctuary, which was different from the rest of the building and I thought looked more like a church, but without all the statues and paintings, it was actually quite empty of religious things. During the demonstration both mediums gave quite convincing messages to people in the audience and the way they did it was again very matter of fact. It seemed to me that they had no doubt that they were communicating information from spirits.

The most amazing thing that happened for me in this week was when I attended a class which involved a man called Len Tatt, who went into a trance and spoke with the voice of a spirit, but it wasn't this that amazed me. It was during this session that I glanced over at Sandy who was sitting beside him at the front of the room when I noticed that her faced began to morph into a different person. The first thing I saw was an old Indian woman who seemed to be overshadowing her it looked like she was practically sitting now where Sandy was. Never had I seen anything this clearly in my life and no sooner had I taken this in when she changed again, this time into an old pagan type woman, almost witchy, with long wild unkempt hair and raged clothes ... but there was a calming feeling accompanying these visions, which totally surprised me. I wondered if what I saw was the medium's spirit guides, but I didn't dare ask for fear of being wrong.

It was the notion that we all have a spirit guide that fascinated me when I first heard this at the College and that set me on a new quest to find mine. It wasn't long before one of the other tutors in my class told me that I had a North American Indian who was guiding me and no sooner had I been told this, than I tried to visualise this entity in my next meditation.

Now, to all intents and purposes I did imagine an Indian man in full feathers, beads and bones, but I began to doubt it because it all happened too easily. Was I making things up just to fit in with the others who seemed to have an amazing array of exotic guides that ranged from Confucius to John the Baptist? I must admit there was a real buzz about being in that atmosphere and meeting all these spiritualist type people, but when I got home my old friend "Doubt" visited me again and again. I think now how normal it is to doubt such experiences because even though there was a highly charged energy in the place that allowed me to see and experience some phenomena, it just didn't feel that I was in the right place yet.

Back in Frankfurt, Gordon was talking to the students about how he met me at one of his book signings and how from that point on he had invited me into his small private home circle and that I had grown in such a short time. Right at that moment I didn't feel the growth he was talking about, instead my mind pulled me to the moment I met my teacher and I remembered being the last one in the line to have books signed along with my friend Paul, when he asked me if I was a medium, or was I in development and how I reacted quick, cocky and saying I was, "the dogs." "It's a bit of cockney rhyming-slang and I won't explain it if you don't mind."

Gordon just laughed at me and asked if I was in a development circle and to my surprise, he joined Paul and I for a drink while the people from his publishers tidied away the rest of the books and things. It was quite something I thought at the time for this guy who was so well known to take time to speak to us and offer us guidance in a very down to earth way. He honestly seemed to be interested in helping us.

The short version of what happened was that he helped us to find a circle with one of his friends, but like my experience at Stansted, I still felt there was something missing in the teaching and I wasn't sure what. It was only when I spoke to Gordon again during a phone conversation that he said he was starting a new circle himself and if I wanted, I could try it out and see if it felt more comfortable. It was the best news I could have gotten at the time because since we first met, I had looked up his work on the internet and found that he was one of the most respected mediums in the country and that he had travelled the world giving lectures and demonstrations to thousands of people and honestly, there were always good comments about him, by scientists, psychologists and many other credible people. I somehow knew in my gut that this was the real next step in my development.

For the next couple of years, Gordon's flat in Pimlico in the centre of London, became my spiritual classroom. There were only three of us who sat in the circle back then, Gordon, his partner Jim, who was a very good healer and of course *yours truly*. I really thought that my mediumship would take off and in no time at all I would be able to give demonstrations of mediumship like Sandy Baker and Glyn Edwards had done at the college and even the way I had seen my teacher do in big crowded rooms full of eager people waiting for messages from the other side. It was nothing like I expected, nothing at all.

Gordon had made me sit and quieten my mind, he tried to teach me not to get messages, but instead just sit in stillness and do nothing and think as little as possible. He said this was all I was expected to do during the one-hour sessions. "I mean seriously, this sought-after medium doesn't do anything during the circle?" It was baffling at first but slowly it began to dawn on me that the more my thinking mind would get quiet and I had no interest in getting messages, that I then started to feel things around my body. It felt like there was a presence close to me in this silence and it was only when I tried to think about it or work out what it was that my mind was back in the room and I was losing the connection with who, or whatever it was. But I began to realise that "it" was what I was looking for and I knew my teacher knew this.

It must have been about a year or so into this sitting in silence practice when I can honestly say that I really sensed and felt the presence of my spirit guide. This was the presence who had been beside me all along and now I was learning not to try to use my brain or my imagination. Both can truly confuse the spiritual student in this type of exercise. I just tried be open to my finer senses and experience the atmosphere around my body, the empty space if you like. That was it, it felt real, it was better than any imaginary picture I had witnessed to that point because I felt it, truly felt the presence and I didn't doubt it. It was real unlike my North American Indian, who I think I just imagined because I was told that was who my guide was. You see, you can imagine most things if you want to, but feeling and sensing take it to a whole other level of sensitivity and reality.

I had been practicing in circle for about two years when Gordon was asked by his publisher to write a book about training mediums to develop their skills and he came up with the idea that he would ask me to contribute my own experiences in his book. He felt that it would benefit the students to hear the words of someone who was still a student himself, but who was just a bit further down the road than they were. It was an honour to do this, the book was to be called *Intuitive Studies* and I was going to write down my own feelings about how I got started to help other people who were looking for spiritual guidance; it really was hard to believe at first.

Writing stories and episodes of the book wasn't the only thing that surprised me around that time, because Gordon also felt that when he was taking workshops and classes with new students who were at the very beginning of their development, he should take me with him and let me get some practise at speaking to the groups and informing them about my development. Again, his thinking was if a brand-new student could see someone who was just a couple of years in and developing well, it was easier for them to aspire to develop mediumship themselves and it would also let them see the progression that could be opened to them if they were truly interested.

That brings me right to this point where I find myself sitting petrified in front of fifty something German students about to put my neck on the line. "Oh, incidentally, that's how I got here!" I was suddenly brought out of my wonderings with the dreaded words coming from my teacher. "Ladies and Gentlemen, let me now introduce you to that student I've been telling you about, Steven Levett ..." As I slowly began to stand up from my chair, I could feel a weight like quick drying cement pour down the inside of my legs. I felt riveted to the spot where I was standing and I remember that my mouth was completely dry now. I knew that I had to walk forward and that I had to speak but my body seemed to be fighting against me when, a thought left my mind like silent words into the air above me, "spirit help me," and just like that I felt my foot lift up and I was taking the first step into my new future.

Throughout this book, as well as telling my own story, I would also like to share some of the exercises with you, which I felt really helped me on my path in the hope that it makes your own journey a little bit clearer. This is the first exercise I was taught in Gordon's circle and I feel it will be helpful to any student who is starting out on the path to spiritual development. For those students who wish to practice the exercises, I suggest that you keep notes of anything you experience after each session. Even if nothing much occurs, it is still good to keep records, as over time you will have a better view of how you are progressing.

**Exercise 1: Sitting in the Silence**

*Correct your posture and your breathing – take a deep breath in through your nose pulling the air* deep down into *your lungs.*

*Feel how your chest expands as it fills with air – now let go of the breath – slowly until you feel your body empty of air* and your *chest is relaxed.*

*Just allow your body to breathe at its own pace now.*

*Focus your attention on your body and register how it feels, using your mind to command the body to RELAX and feel the weight of your body supported by the chair and the floor beneath you.*

*Be aware of the rhythm of your breathing becoming slower and as it slows you will become more relaxed.*

*Notice that you are now on a mind level, aware of your relaxed body and not being disturbed by needless thoughts or concerns.*

*You are clear and must be still and quiet in both body and mind ... sit in this silence.*

*Keeping your focus on this peaceful state helps you to empty yourself of small things. Things which might normally irritate you; clear all disturbances from your mind.*

*Be as still as you can and keep the mind clear because it is a sacred-space. Stay in this sacred space peaceful and calm ever observing the atmosphere around you, but not trying to accomplish or achieve anything.*

*Remain in this state until you feel ready to bring your mind back to your waking consciousness and you can do this by once again inhaling deep breathes into your body allowing the brain to become more alert and awake.*

*Stretch your body and shake yourself awake...*

This first, very simple meditation is essential to everything that comes after. For me, this exercise became my regular practice; it really helped me to clear all the nonsense out of my mind and now when I sit in my circle, I try to achieve this state of a quiet mind before moving on to anything else.

# 3.
# PATIENCE

*Patience is a virtue they say, but it takes a heck of a long time to get it.*

I was once told that if something is worth having, then it is worth waiting for. It was like when I started out in my apprenticeship as a painter, I thought I would learn everything in a year tops and be working on the tools and earning great money. How wrong I was, in fact my total time in training lasted almost five years and during that time I was often used as a general dogsbody by the guys who were qualified – so much for my quick thinking!

I had actually signed up for a three-year course in this trade and even when I finished that, I once again thought I had arrived – but not so. When my apprenticeship was over I went into my first job and the foreman asked if I had completed my college training and when I told him I had, he replied, "well, forget everything you've just learned, it means nothing here." Talk about being crestfallen, I was totally devastated.

The same thing happened to me when I first went to develop my mediumship with Gordon. I had been learning from different people and taken myself off to places like The Arthur Findlay College, not to mention all the books I had read and lectures I had attended; it was like painting all over again.
Gordon listened to all my endeavours and spiritual and psychic experiences and I honestly thought he would be impressed, but just like the foreman on my first job he said, "OK, let's put that to one side and concentrate on what you need to learn." Honestly, these people ...

I really look back at both those experiences and appreciate them now, first because my first foreman made me a much better painter, he helped me to turn theory into good practice and with Gordon, he helped to guide me from what I thought I wanted to do, to what I am doing now with great confidence; honestly, these people!

To this point I always believed that my direction in the spiritual world was to be a medium. In fact, I was so convinced by this because of the episodes like sensing my nan when she gave me the information about my mum looking at her ring. And also, there was one time when I saw my Granddad one night when I was just sitting watching television in my parents' living room, both my parents were there at the time, so there was nothing spiritual or psychic happening, I thought. But out of nowhere I saw a television screen appear above the actual set and it was as real as the original. Both my parents were completely unaware of this happening, which made the whole thing seem very bizarre. I looked at both of them for a moment and I was certain that this apparition was only for me. On the screen I saw my Granddad standing, he appeared from the waist up, he was wearing a white vest, which I thought peculiar as I had never seen him wear such a thing before. He had always been the kind of man who dressed well and was conscientious enough that he would not let his family see him half dressed. Even more peculiar than this was that he was wearing bright red braces, something I had never seen him wear in my life.

The quality of this vision was so strong and realistic that he appeared animated like he was alive in some sort of way, not like a still photograph at all. Behind my grandfather was a caravan and a fence that was made of white and cream overlapping panels. Again, the reality of this image was almost in high definition. I was so shocked and slightly jolted on the sofa where I was lying, my father never even noticed this, but my mum who was aware of my psychic development at the time turned to me and gave me a look that told me she was picking up on my feelings. Mum got off her seat and turned to me and gave me a look to indicate that she wanted me to follow her, so I duly did. In the kitchen she asked me straight out, "What did you see?' At first, I was taken aback because I thought she might have seen the same thing but it was clear that she hadn't from the way she looked, very puzzled and questioning. "I saw granddad," was the first thing I said.

She examined my face and I knew she wanted me to tell her more. “He was wearing a white vest and really bright red braces, which didn’t make sense to me.” I told her; I could tell by her expression that it didn’t make much sense to her either. “He was standing in front of a caravan with a white and cream fence…” “Oh yeah, I know that caravan and granddad always wore his vest like that on holiday, it was when we went to Hastings, you were just a baby at the time Steve, but the red braces, I honestly don’t think he ever wore braces, especially red braces.” I could see some doubt appear on her face and her excitement began to dissipate. I felt uncomfortable because I was so certain what I had seen and my mum was quite excited about what I was telling her, now it all felt quite doubtful. The things I had told her before always seemed quite exact and though all the other details were right, this one doubt cast a shadow that touched us both. Mum left the kitchen with doubt written all over her face and I could tell she was searching her memory to find this small detail, but my stomach was turning because I had a sense that it wasn’t over.

For the rest of the evening, she sat with her eyes on the telly, but her mind in the past. My gut was pushing me to do something and I wasn't sure what, but no sooner had I had that thought when I was impressed to look for the old family photo albums. I went to the cabinet where all the family albums were and I began to sift through them; it was one of those times when you feel like you are on a mission. Page after page I turned until there it was, a picture of granddad lying down on a sun-stretcher, in white vest in front of the caravan with white and cream stripped fence, though at first glance, no red braces. I looked at the picture and scrutinised it, as is my way, (I'm a Virgo,) and there it was between his waist and his elbow a small portion of a bright red brace sticking out like a sore thumb. "Eureka!" I knew I had to follow my gut, my intuition wouldn't let this one go, I was like a dog with a bone and rightly so.

My dad was going off to bed when I called mum back into the kitchen to reveal my findings and as she approached me, I said. "Mum, look what I found?" I held out the picture in front of her face and at first like me she saw the man lying in the white vest in front of the said caravan and stuff and then her eyes, like mine fell on the small portion of colour that stood out. "Gordon-Bennett!!!" That's cockney for "I can't believe it." She was stunned, as I was. Her excitement had returned and I told her that at the end of the original vision I had witnessed I had heard my granddad say. "Remember me like this, not like I was at the end." Mum told me that, that holiday was one of the best memories she could remember having with her father.

So for me, I honestly assumed because of such experiences, mediumship seemed to be a natural path to go down. The one thing I've learned about the spiritual path is that the only true certainty is that nothing is certain. During my first visit to the Arthur Findlay College, the medium, Len Tatt was standing outside the canteen waiting to get in line for food just beside me when he turned to me and said, "Do you know that you would make a great healer?" This came totally out of nowhere and I was left standing not knowing quite what to say as I watched him move away from me. I felt a bit shocked that he singled me out when I hadn't been in his classes at that point, but also because I didn't really have a clue what he meant because I hadn't even looked into healing. I was totally into developing my mediumship, so I suppose I even felt a bit deflated to be honest.

Having put Len's comments to the back of my mind, I was sauntering down one of the long corridors in the college when one of the female tutors came walking towards me with a huge grin on her face. She gave me the impression that she was hearing something in the empty space around her head. "I mean, Hogwarts or what?" I hadn't had any dealings with this woman but I had seen her with the other tutors on the platform on the opening night during the introduction. "Ah yes, you would make a fine healer, I've just been told, young man." This had to be some sort of psychic conspiracy I was thinking. The strange woman walked past me and carried on down the corridor in the opposite direction behind me before I even got a chance to open my mouth and as I looked around me, I realised that I was the only person there, so she had to be talking to me. A part of me hoped that there would have been someone else behind me but there wasn't and again I was left with the feeling of disappointment because it would seem that these mediums and tutors were pointing my development in the opposite direction from where I wanted it to go.

In Gordon's circle where I thought I was doing well and getting to learn slowly as he had instructed me, after telling me to put all the previous development to one side, I was shocked again when he told me I should start to practice healing with Jim once a week as he thought it would be good for me... At first, I thought about protesting but I knew that after only being in this small circle for just over a year I had already learned much more about development than during all the years that had gone before. So, I sucked it up and did what I was told, remembering the words of Len Tatt and the woman who talks to mid-air and wondering if they were actually talking sense.

It was strange for me because I had already been taught that some of the things I had learned in my previous attempts to grow spiritually were no more than my imagination; like the time I was told by a medium I had a North American Indian guide, which after being told such, I duly invented. "I didn't want to be the only boy at the spiritual party without a guide..."
No, my new teacher made me go slow and examine everything that came into my mind, he made me question what I was seeing and investigate things to find out if they had any real relevance or was it all just fantasy ... A bit frustrating at the start, but a year or so down the line I had learned how to sense the presence of spirit and recognise the fantasies which the mind can throw at you when you first start to practice meditation.

It was my new teacher who told me that it wasn't important to get messages. In fact, he said he didn't want to hear them if I did get them because he says I was nowhere near ready to do such things and I genuinely trusted his good sense and no-nonsense approach to spiritual development. It was also very reassuring that he didn't seem to get messages in the circle which did surprise me, but he would tell me that was not the purpose of our circle and that I would know when the time was right what direction my development would be taking. At this point I didn't but I knew I was changing somehow. Instead of getting fantastic messages and images in my mind, I felt a sort of inner peace and also, I was losing the need to try to see things and get messages, though my attitude was changing and my ability to sense energy in the room was becoming much more heightened. There was a true feeling of everything slowing down and my eager mind was following this pattern; the rush to be something psychic had left me and I think I started to develop patience. It was then that I sensed the presence of my spirit guide and he wasn't some big Indian Chief in full feathers, beads and bones. I say this because I had since been taught to stop looking for images of guides and just try to feel the atmosphere around me and if I learned to do this, I would feel the essence of the spirit who was guiding me and in learning to feel the essence, I would soon be able to interpret the feelings and describe them in much better detail.

This I did and I was so moved by the sensations I would pick up whenever spirit where close to me. It was different from the visions that I had earlier because the sense of spirit filled me and left me with no doubt that I had experienced something, whereas when I saw pictures in my mind, I could never be sure if what I was seeing was coming from the spirit world or my imagination. It was also at this time I learned that each time my guide would come close to me I would pick up the same feeling. It was like his signature if you like, his way of letting me know that he was near. Gordon called it *the Calling Card* and he explained to me that all the time I sat in his circle he was waiting for me to feel this and it is only when I told him what it was like that, he confirmed it and he knew then that I was ready to move on to the next episode in my development and then it meant healing.

Each week, in the group I would be given instructions on healing, but it was clear to Jim from the very outset that I was a natural. The first session where he asked me to do healing on him, I felt an enormous amount of heat pouring through my hands as I rested them on his shoulders. Once again, there was an actual feeling that something was happening. Even with my questioning brain I found it hard not to accept that "something" was there when a person's hands would get hotter by touching someone else's body – but it was the "volume" of heat which astounded me. The other thing I was aware of was that Jim would be almost asleep by the end of the session and would often comment that the overwhelming power coming through me was putting him into a sort of trance state. I was truly loving the experiences because there was an effect and I knew I couldn't be making this up and before long I had left the thought of mediumship to one side, just as I had been asked to do.

There was something amazing about the sensation of healing someone and more than that. I began to read up on some of the great spiritualist healers of the past like Nan McKenzie, a woman from Yorkshire, who worked for years as a healer in London and who cured thousands of people with her gift, and Harry Edwards who did the same. There was so much to learn and so many gifted people to look up to and learn about. I wanted to absorb it all into my mind about the great healers and it seemed that every time I did, I felt spurred on to learn more and practice more.

Twice a week now I would visit Gordon and Jim's flat, one Sunday night for our regular circle where I was learning to develop a stronger link with the spirit world and each Wednesday to practice healing with Jim. Sometimes Gordon would sit in to watch how I was doing and somehow this didn't bother me because I trusted the feelings and the contact from the spirit world much more than I had before. In fact, I think I could say that it was at this time when I really began to get comfortable in myself with what I was learning, something had shifted and it felt right and though I still had episodes of mediumship ahead of me, healing was what made me feel at peace with myself. After all the uncertainties and doubt I had in myself I was starting to relax and understand that I needed to struggle along my path to reach this place of peace. I said at the very beginning of this chapter, "If something is worth having, it's worth waiting for!" and now I think I can say I truly believe this because I have experienced it!

# 4.

# Spirit Guides

I hadn't really thought about spirit guides or guardians, who watch over us until I had made my first trip to the Arthur Findlay College, but it's the kind of thing that once you are made aware of it; you are interested to find out if you have one. For me it became a focus of my attention for a while at the end of my first training course, but after some time the notion sort of faded, that is until I began to sit in circle.

I can remember asking my circle companions whether they knew who their guides were and noted that neither seemed to sound that excited as they answered and said they did, but just sort of brushed it aside. I found it strange that they would know such a thing but not be eager to talk about it, how bizarre? Outside of Spiritualism or mediumship, I suppose not many people would even understand the term "spirit guide," but it still kind of intrigued me to learn more about them and how I could get to know more about this Red Indian chief who I had been told was my guide. I have explained that in circle, I was made to still my mind and learn how to dull down my thinking and this was how I learned to sense the atmosphere around me during my meditation practise and instead of focussing my attention n on me and what goes on in my inner thinking and imagination, I honestly started to feel a pressure outside of me, a sort of presence, something, which I hadn't been aware of before.

It was around a year after I had first been invited to sit in the circle that I began to lose touch with my thoughts. I would find myself in a sort of in-between state, neither focussed on one thing or another, my awareness was really on my breath and the slow rhythm my body would pulsate at when my breathing became so slow. Then I would begin to sense a presence beside me, like someone was actually standing there. I had sensed the presence of unseen forces before, but in this controlled environment with my two friends it appeared to be stronger, much more exaggerated.

While I would sense this presence, I would also notice that there was a sensation on my face, like static electricity always on the same left cheek and always at the same time as the invisible force became very pronounced at my left side. At the end of these sessions my teacher would ask me what I felt and I would describe it as I have just done. He would nod his head and not say much in response, which usually left me feeling baffled, but the experience of sitting in that kind of energy or atmosphere always made me feel good and not so keen to question; it was just like "all was well."

I believe that as we develop spiritually our need to ask questions seems to fade, well, it did for me during our weekly sessions. It was when I had been sitting in the circle for around two years that I realised the presence I was sensing in my weekly practice was my spirit guide and it was then that Gordon gave me the confirmation that I needed to understand this.
One night just before we all closed our eyes to meditate, he said to me, "Steven, when you feel that presence

tonight send out one thought and ask if this is your guide."
I wondered what he meant, but somehow, I understood and then he told me that the sensation on my face would come in response to my question and when it did, I should ask the guide to remove it and see what followed.

I did what I was asked and during the session I felt the strong sensation of a person standing to my left so I asked if this was my guide and an immediate response happened: I felt the electrical charge on my left cheek. I asked in my mind if the guide could remove this sensation and immediately it was not there. Now, that was all I was asked to do, but me being me, I asked for the feeling to be brought back and it was and again I asked for it to be removed and again it was. I don't know how many times in all I asked this but it was certainly much more than once.

The experience was quite exciting because it felt like I was being answered by an intelligence. And even more than that there was a familiarity there and I could have sworn

that the presence I could feel was happy; like there was an advancement or progression of some kind that brought a feeling of joy to this first-contact.
That evening we sat talking till late. I was elated and I knew in the very heart of me that I had felt an invisible force in the empty space around me that I conversed with and who answered me. I learned that my guide had been building a stronger presence around me for a while and each week was making a more powerful link with me and this night my teacher sensed that I should reach out and ask something, as he had a very sure feeling that it was time for me to take my next step in my development.

For me this was quite amazing. I didn't see fanciful visions of Crazy Horse, my made-up guide, nor did I get any great messages; in fact, what happened might appear very simple, but it felt authentic. Since my early experiences of wondering and even making up ideas of spirit guides, I really wanted to be able to validate the real thing when it happened and because of the simple and clear guidance I had been given, I felt I could say that this was genuine, a true experience which I could build on.

I was taught that in the old days of mediumship, spirit would sometimes make rapping noises in response to questions people put to them, so if the spirit force was communicating you would ask a question and ask them to make one noise for yes and two for no etc. What I had experienced was similar and now I thought I had a system to test the spirit who works with me.
From then until now I still ask my guide to use this simple and effective system if I need to get guidance from spirit, but since then my link has grown and I have been given clairvoyant pictures of what my guide looked like when he was in the physical life, information which I have looked into and found to be true. It is this kind of investigation that when it bears fruit and can be validated, it gives the spiritual student more trust in their spiritual guides. We should always test our guides until we have some kind of proof, remember you are dealing with a very intelligent and evolved consciousness.

I feel that who and what my spirit guide means to me is quite personal, so I don't divulge too much information about what happens between us. But I can tell my students how to try to contact their guide and build a trust which they can help to strengthen their belief and connection.  I understand now why my circle companions didn't want to say so much to me about their own guides when I had asked if they were aware of them, they simply did not want to influence my mind or thinking.

You see, there is a lot more which happens in the spirit world with our guides than we know and if the guide is the teacher, they should slowly unfold the relevant information for the student when it is right for them. Often people can be led into very fanciful ideas and non-realities when it comes to spirit guides.  It is my understanding that the guide is there throughout your life, even if you are never aware of it. I do feel that if you open up spiritually and start on a path of spiritual progression that the guide will make themselves known to you when you are truly ready and not a moment sooner. I believe if you see who the guide was when they were in the physical life, that there is a teaching in that. For example, if the image of the guide was in the form of a Catholic nun, then maybe the person they are guiding should also look at the archetype and symbolism and learn to be more devoted or contemplative. If you learn maybe about the order this nun represented you might find out more about her earthly practice and there might be a lesson you could follow in your life at that moment; and so on.

I also believe that when, and only when, you are ready to work and understand the purpose of your spirit guide that they will introduce you to other levels of spiritual teaching and again maybe different archetypes might be shown to you to learn more lessons to add to your spiritual expansion. But we have only one guide and sometimes other teachers.

People should be careful not to over-imagine that every vision they see or thought of a certain archetype is a guide, sometimes we do just imagine things but if you develop properly and make a proper and authentic contact with your guide, they will help to steer you, as the term "Guide" suggests. My teacher chose not to put ideas into my mind, instead he let me experience the phenomena when I was ready and in my own way. He knew who my guide was and what was needed to help me make that contact clearly and easily without any drama and that is how I try to lead people in return now.

I feel that my guide is like my eyes and ears in the spirit world, a loving force who helps me to help other people. But I certainly don't think spirit should be used as a cosmic commodity to solve all of your life's problems or give solutions to all of your doubts and fears. No, this life is ours to experience and I feel very guided, but when things occur in my life and I am faced with choices then I have to do this on my own and take responsibility for my decisions. Though, no matter what I choose or how things turn out, I do feel that the spirit around me will always support me.

Remember, other people may understand spirit guides very differently but I share with you my own feelings of what a guide is and what it means to me. What I will say is that each time I am asked to heal people I feel that strong presence of my guide beside me and when I do the results are always honest and true. The type of spirit healing I practice is working with the energy of my guide channelling through me so to be able to feel the presence is all I need to begin my work. If I don't have this feeling at the start then I know that it is not time for healing.

In some way I believe we are connected with our guides from another time and this is why the presence feels familiar, and in some other way I think we have made a pact or contract to support each other through different experiences of life, whether in this physical world or in the spirit world – and at this time one is here and the other overseeing from a higher realm.

I am certainly happy that I have my connection to my guide and I can only truly advise those still searching to go slow and be true to yourself in the process; there is a great reassurance in knowing that in this world we are never truly alone.

**Exercise 2: The Calling Card**

*Begin the same way as the previous exercise and correct your posture and your breathing – take a deep breath in through your nose pulling the air deep down into your lungs.*

*Feel how your chest expands as it fills with air – now let go of the breath – slowly until you feel your body empty of air and your chest is relaxed.*

*Just allow your body to breathe at its own pace now.*

*Focus your attention on your body and register how it feels: using your mind to command the body to RELAX and feel the weight of your body supported by the chair and the floor beneath you.*

*Be aware of the rhythm of your breathing becoming slower and as it slows you will become more relaxed.*

*Notice that you are now on a mind level, aware of your relaxed body and not being disturbed by needless thoughts or concerns.*
*You are clear and must be still and quiet in both body and mind – sit in the silence. Keeping your focus on this peaceful state helps you to empty yourself of small things. Things which might normally irritate you; clear all disturbance from your mind.*
*Be as still as you can and keep the mind clear because it is a sacred space. Stay in this sacred space peaceful and calm, ever observing the atmosphere around you, but not trying to accomplish or achieve anything.*
*From the quiet of your mind send out one thought: welcome your guide into your sacred space and wait.*

*Try to feel any change in the atmosphere around you, notice any sensations which occur on or near the body. Register feelings but don't allow your thinking mind to take over, this is about feeling and sensing more than thinking. Make no attempt at this point to analyse what is happening, rather just experience and make no attempt to understand at this point.*

*Sit like this for a bit until you feel that you have been able to sense the changes around you. Then you may send out a second thought, which is to ask the guide to step out of your space.*

*Start to breathe more deliberately and begin to bring your awareness back to the room. Wait until you feel totally focussed, then stretch out your arms and move your fingers around to get all the blood circulating in your body. Stand up for a moment and stretch your body before sitting down again.*

*Now just try to recall, first the most prominent change which you felt when asking the guide to join you. Try to be clear when recalling the sensations you experienced. This exercise helps you to learn to experience sensations and feelings without over analysing or fantasising. If there was something that stands out more than others, just remember it, neither add nor take away anything, let it be.*

It is so important at this time for students not to allow their mind to invent things. This is what I did when I was told that I had an Indian as my guide. The difference with this practice is that you are asked not to apply thought, but learn to just experience. When you have had the chance to practice this exercise several times you might find that there is a definite sensation which you feel only when you ask your guide to be present; and for me this was a tingling feeling which moved over one side of my face, almost like static electricity. Now whenever I work as a healer, I always experience this sensation and that has become the "calling card" of my spirit guide. It is what lets me know that it is alright to work, it's our code if you like. It was often explained to me in my early development, "feeling is believing." I find this so helpful as unlike imagery and thinking, which often serve to confuse, the feeling happens on, or in the body and therefore you know how real it is.

# 5.

# THE PRACTICE

*It is often said that*

*practice makes perfect*

*but for me practice has*

*become a way of life.*

If anyone would have said to me when I was growing up in South London that I would be a practicing healer, I would honestly have laughed in their face. This whole idea of changing my mind-set from a likely lad to spiritual healer was at first very daunting. There is such a massive difference in being asked to go round someone's house to price a job and sitting with a person or family in some cases to ask them how I can bring healing to them, and give reassurance about difficult situations in their life.

I had given healing to people in my circle and these were all people who had a knowledge about the spirit world and all of them had some understanding of the healing arts. But when I first had to do this on one of the general public, I was really beginning to wonder what the hell I was doing. I was often faced with my own self-doubt in the early days and no more so when I was asked by Gordon to go the home of a lady he knew who was suffering with chronic back pain and who was desperate to have some healing after having injections of cortisone which it appeared were having little affect.

Here I was, walking down the streets of Mayfair, a far cry from the Elephant and Castle in South London, looking for this apartment and feeling like turning back and thinking of calling my friend and asking him if I could do it another day. Something inside kept me walking through Berkeley Square looking at the amazing buildings, yet not exactly taking in the splendour of LondonW1. I remember my heart sinking and my stomach churning when I came to the apartment block of the client and suddenly realised that all my inner protests meant nothing now and all I could do was to press the intercom to apartment 10a.

I shuddered and took a step back when almost at once a strong American female voice echoed out at me. "Hello, Stevie, is that you?" I somehow managed to blurt out. "Yeah."

"Come on up." There was something in her voice that seemed to ease my nervousness, she sounded friendly and I headed up the beautifully decorated stairway whose carpets must have been two inches thick. I arrived on the second floor to be greeted by a woman in her fifties with short brown close-cut hair and a smile so bright with the whitest teeth I think I'd ever seen in my life.

"Hi honey, thank you so much for seeing me at such short notice." She said, and again I began to relax at her easy manner. "Yeah, no problem, this is a really nice place." "Well, its home, but nothing seems nice when your back is breaking." She let her hand fall behind her lower back to the place I assumed she was feeling the pain and in a second, I almost felt a shock of pain touch my own back. The short version of this was that I began the healing and

even though I knew she had a bad back, during the healing session I felt like my own body had somehow taken on all her pain and I'm not gonna lie, but it was absolutely killing me. I honestly had never felt pain like it. It felt like someone was pushing a hot poker into my spine, but for some reason I had to keep going and all the time I was healing her in agonising pain, she kept on talking.
"I travel so much I suppose I brought this on myself, I know I should slow down, but it's just so hard to say no to work right now."

"Talk about rabbit, rabbit, rabbit." She did go on...

At the end of the session, she turned to me and gave me such a funny look before she spoke. "Oh my God, I can't feel anything?" She stood up and put both her hands behind her and still looking weird she said. "Wow." My own back was still breaking and she looked like she had won the lottery. She was laughing now and still I felt the pain in my lower back, but didn't say anything because it was starting to ease and somehow, I knew in my gut that it would leave me, but all the while I kept it to myself.

What I was experiencing were the conditions; this is what some healers say when they take on a person's pain sympathetically. The only time I had ever heard of this kind of thing was when I heard one of my mates joking about taking on his wife's labour pains when she was pregnant, but healers I had met had told me that they quite often absorbed the pain of the patient, especially when the pain was severe, which this lady's must have been.

As I was leaving, she kept trying to give me money and gifts for what I had done for her, but I really didn't want to take anything from her, I still felt like a bit of a novice and she was a friend of a friend and I honestly had never thought about charging people money for healing, after all it wasn't like I'd just painted her kitchen or anything. No, this all felt different and certainly not like the work I was used to doing.

By the time I got back to the tube station at Charing Cross the phantom pain had left me and something about the whole experience had lifted me and made me feel quite good about what I had just done.

I remember sitting on the tube on my way home looking at people across from me and wondering if some of them were in pain or suffering depressions or some kind of stress, or loss and I realised that they all probably had something wrong with them on one level or another and all of a sudden, I thought of how many people could benefit from what I could do. It was my first time healing a member of the public, but I knew it wouldn't be my last.

It was about two weeks after my encounter with the American lady that I found myself travelling to see a patient this time in Basel, yes Switzerland! I was helping to run a class on spiritual development, which included exercises in mediumship and healing when one of the students asked me if I would be able to do some healing on her at the end of the class.

It was one of those funny moments when you get a strong feeling in your gut when a person talks to you. This always happens to me when I know that I have to do healing on a person, so very quickly I agreed to see her. She was a good-looking woman somewhere in her fifties I suspected, but the most obvious thing about her was her eyes; they were brown in colour but there was a look that told me she was holding a very deep sadness inside and I believe that was what triggered my funny feeling that she really needed help.

I was still quite new to all this, but I was learning things about my healing practice, such as the type of healing I did on the American woman was very hands-on and more physical, but with this Swiss lady who I believed was suffering emotionally, my hands never touched her at all. Instead, I was quite amazed that there was a strong force lifting my arms above her body and my hands were making passes over her head. There was a moment when I realised that I had no idea how long the healing had gone on for and with that conscious thought I felt that it was over.

I stood in front of this woman who was still sitting on her chair with her eyes closed. Though it was plain that tears were streaming down her cheeks, yet her body was motionless, like she was in a kind of trance. I didn't try to wake her, again it was instinctive, like the movement of my hands during the healing. Instead, I just waited patiently for her to come back and when she did, she looked astonished. I got a sense that she also had a strange lapse of time or something because she shook her head and blinked her eyes a few times before speaking and when she did, she simply said "Wow!"

Her next response was to stand up and put her arms around me saying. "Thank you, thank you so much." I honestly didn't know how to respond and kind of shrugged embarrassedly. "Yeah, no problem, how are you feeling luv?" I said, not really knowing what else to say. It pains me to think how shy I was back then, something else

I have had to get over. I waited for her to continue. "Great, I feel like something has been lifted off my shoulders and I don't know how to explain it."

It was at the very end of this session, just before she opened her eyes that I got the impression that this woman was grieving and for a split second I thought I saw a young boy in his teens standing behind her; I couldn't be sure so I didn't mention it to her after all, she asked me for healing, not a message from the other side, I left that stuff to real mediums, but I was almost certain that I had seen this child standing beside her.

In the end I felt it was best not to ruin the good moment by speaking about the spirit child or anything because from my point this lady looked happier than when she first sat down and as a healer, I really felt that my work was done.  It wasn't until the following day that I got my answer, though actually I had forgotten already all about it. Gordon was giving a demonstration of mediumship for the students on our course and my patient got the first message from her teenage son who was in the spirit world

and so pleased to come through and pass positive messages to his mother.
I couldn't believe it, the way he was being described was just like the child I had seen the previous day, though I never picked up on how he died or his characteristics like the medium was doing now. Still, it touched me in a strange way to know that what I saw was now being validated by my friend and more than this, his mother looked elated to hear from her boy.

I hadn't really mentioned what happened during the healing to Gordon simply because I wasn't a hundred percent certain if what I was seeing was real or my imagination, but after the demonstration I had to talk about it and get some feedback from my teacher about what I saw. The strange thing was he had no problem believing or understanding what I had experienced, in fact he said that when he used to do healing for people who were grieving, that often he would see their spirit family and on occasion even get messages from them. I had seen spirit forms and had messages when I was younger and though now my development was more concentrated on healing;

I was beginning to understand that when you were open spiritually, that all things were possible and now I was beginning to feel that my gift was opening further and it was actually better that I didn't say anything to Gordon because through the message he gave to the woman I really got a clear answer which might never have happened if I had spoken about it.

It was at the end of our Basel trip that I realised how much my healing was growing and even though I had been taught in my development about how to practice my skill, that with each new healing, new experiences were occurring. I was definitely noticing the difference in how my hands would move when a person was in physical pain to the way they did when the patient was suffering emotionally. Also, the *loss of time* thing I was explained was more like trance healing when the spirit guide takes more control of the healer's body and mind and what was really great about this was how practical the experiences were. No book or lecture I had learned from could teach me like this, there was a great excitement building in me about my healing practice and I loved it.

The number of patients I was seeing was growing and only from word of mouth and also because I was taking part in the workshops with my teacher who would push me forward whenever a person asked about healing; he felt that nothing was a better teacher in this field than practical experience and I was beginning to see that he was right.

Back in London almost a year on from the time I was asked to see the American woman I was back assisting in a workshop near Euston Station. We had a group of about thirty students all interested in learning about spiritual development and keen to practice the exercises Gordon had used to develop me and was now using all over Europe.

Always when he would explain that just three years ago Steven was kind of lost in his development and now he's a working healer and helps teach the same development that helped him to grow, people would want to ask me questions, usually in the coffee or lunch breaks and almost always there would be someone who would ask if I could do some healing on them.

It was on this very hot summer day in London when I was standing outside the hall we were using, having a chat with one of the students, when I became aware that a small slim woman was standing close by waiting to speak to me. “Steven, I’m sorry to disturb you, but do you have a place where you practice your healing, only I would love to come to you and see if you can help me?”

As it happened, I didn’t have a clinic or special place to do my healings and in fact I did explain to the woman that I only did them when I was either in workshops or if someone wanted me to come to their home. “I don’t live in London.” She said and then looked at me with eyes that where almost pleading. “Well unless you want me to see if we can use the workshop room at the end of the day?” It was really what she wanted and her expression changed immediately. I knew Gordon would not have a problem with this as he was the one who always encouraged me to practice as often as I could and he hardly took notice of me when I told him about the woman's request. "Yes sure, that fine." I think he said something like that.

Anyway, at the end of the workshop I led the little woman towards the far corner of the room where I had set out a chair for her to sit. It was strange because I often found myself just telling people to relax and that I would begin by placing my hands on their shoulders and at the end of the healing session I would do the same and that way they would know it was over. But this time I don't think I said anything, it just happened that the lady sat down and immediately closed her eyes in a way that told me she had had healing before. I didn't disturb her quiet, instead I gently placed my hands on her very bony shoulders and in the same way as the healing I did for the Swiss lady, my hands sort of floated lightly in the air above the woman's head.

This was different, I could feel physical things happening in my own body. I got a strong sense that the left side of my chest was very uncomfortable, like something was lodged behind the muscle. I didn't really know how to describe it in detail because I also felt very nervous in my stomach and quite exhausted, as if someone had just drained my energy and my hands and arms that were so light and floaty began to feel like they were covered in quick drying cement. There was a part of me that wanted to stop, but something inside kept me going and with that thought of going on, the conditions I was feeling in and around my body faded, only now I saw in my mind's eye what looked like an x-ray of a person's upper body, but it appeared to be clear.

My hands had moved down from above the patient's head and were positioned one in front of her chest area but several inches from her body and the other the same distance from her back – between the hands there was immense heat, I think more that I had ever felt before. It got very strange for me because I could have sworn I heard a voice in my head saying. “It’s all clear”.  Now I was beginning to build a picture in my mind what might be troubling this person, but healers are not doctors and making diagnosis on someone is a big NO NO for me. Also giving a person false hope would be another NO NO; remember I didn’t even ask the woman what she wanted healing for, but I really did hear those words but knew I could never say them when the healing was over.

When the healing was over, I simply asked her if she was ok and she didn’t speak much, but nodded her head in a way to show me she was becoming more aware and awake as I hadn’t realised she had really been knocked out during the session.

It was such a strange experience because she thanked me and left really quickly like she was in a big hurry, leaving me wondering what all the things I was feeling were about. I honestly wanted to ask her about her own condition just for confirmation on what I was picking up, but she wasn’t having any of it. No, she was off like a shot. “How did the healing go then?” Gordon asked me as he

walked back into the seminar room. "I don't actually know," was the way I replied and then I started to try to explain the heavy conditions and the x-ray and the voice etc. "You didn't say any of this to her?" he asked me looking quite worried that his student would have broken such a fundamental rule of healing. "No, I didn't have the chance to say anything to her – she shot off as soon as it was done."
"Oh well, sometimes we are not meant to know things, some healing is done and then forgotten; let's get out of here." We both left the room and headed to the nearby train station.

It puzzled me for a long time what was going on in that healing until one time during another workshop in London one of the former students from the previous time was there and couldn't wait to tell me. "Steven, Jackie says thank you so much for the healing you did for her last time." Who was Jackie I was thinking and looking very perplexed? "You know she had to run for her train and didn't even say goodbye or thanks, but she told me to tell

you that she got the *all clear*." It suddenly dawned on me that this was my strange healing session with the lady who ran, and where I heard the word "It's all clear." I was about to speak but didn't get a chance.
"She thought she had breast cancer and was due to go for a screening the following week. She was so tired and scared in fact she was completely drained with exhaustion with all the worrying she had done, but she wants you to know that the healing gave her energy and really calmed her down."

I really didn't know what to say because there was no point in saying anything to this woman about what happened with her friend, but again something deep inside of me was delighted. Not only because the patient had great news about her health, but also because I couldn't believe that during the session the spirit world were showing me a clear picture and also that I actually took in all, even if it be only for seconds, the very condition this woman was feeling at the time. I have always been quite a doubter and someone who needs proof after proof, but after all the recent results and experiences I had gotten with my healing in the past years I can genuinely say that I was running out of things to doubt, only myself at times, but never the spirit world now.

**Exercise 3: Sitting in the Power**

*Just as in the earlier exercises, begin by fixing your posture and breathing. Take your mind into the silence and allow yourself to relax into this state.*

*If thoughts start to appear in your mind, be aware of them but do not follow them, simply let them be. By practising sitting in the silence regularly you will find that after a while you will be able to manage your lack of thinking much better. Using now the same intention as we did in the "calling card" exercise, send out a thought of welcome to your spirit guide, giving them permission to link with your sacred space and wait to feel the sensation that lets you know that you are in the presence of the higher spirit who works with you.*

*Be still and sit in this energy without sending out any thoughts to achieve or accomplish anything. Learning to sit in the power of spirit will help you with your work as a medium or healer as you develop. It is important to recognise when you are truly in the spirit energy and not just in some fantasy of thought. Always be aware of the feelings of the energy around you without over-analysing it. This experience also allows you to get to know and build a stronger connection with your guide at such a simple level.*

*When you feel the need, ask the guide to step out of your energy and start to bring yourself back as before, breathing in more air to wake your mind and focus on the room, before stretching, standing and grounding yourself again.*

*Take a little time to reflect on things you felt and experienced during the session. This is the time to use your thinking mind, after the experience not during it, again this is another bit of you taking control and training the mind, rather than letting the think run away with you.*

Learning to take control of the thinking mind is part of the development process. So many students ask how they can know the difference between what they personally think and what is really coming from the spirit world. Well, this process of exercises starts with mindfulness of self and then learning to take in what is happening in your immediate atmosphere which includes the subtle energies of the spirit. Don't be in a rush to accomplish at this stage of your journey, it is much better to take it slow and enjoy and get to trust the process.

# 6.

# TRUST

*So many big advances in our lives are born out of moments when we have to trust an unseen power to guide our next footstep on the unseen path into what we call our future.*

There are so many times in our lives we use the word "trust" without truly understanding its proper meaning. In my own life and even without knowing it, I had always tried to look for the safe road and do what all my mates were doing and never really break with what we believed to be the normal. It wasn't until I was part way through my spiritual training that I got to experience what it meant to trust the spirit world and especially my own guides at a whole new level.

I had been practising my healing for a couple of years when I went with Gordon to Sweden where he was leading a workshop on *Developing Mediumship*. I had at this point overcome my initial nervousness of speaking in public when we worked in Germany, and though I still got butterflies in my stomach I didn't feel sick anymore. If anything, I was beginning to enjoy the experiences of sharing what I was learning from my circle and the spirit world with new students who were as keen and eager to learn as I had been at the start of my own journey. If my development has shown me anything, it is that whenever the ground beneath you feels solid and safe and then if you are to advance, things will soon shift and you will be forced to take a step in a new direction. That is exactly what happened to me in Sweden when, just as I was enjoying my new comfort zone of teaching the healing exercises to the beginners which had truly helped me to build some confidence in me and my abilities, Gordon offered me a chance to get on the platform with him to give a demonstration of mediumship.   Suddenly my solid floor started to feel like quicksand and once again I was facing that sinking feeling.

I had originally started my spiritual training with mediumship as my main objective, and though I was still trying to develop as a medium, healing had really become my main practice and something which I focussed my mind much more on now. But my teacher wanted to give me an exercise in "trust." "How much do you truly trust your guides, Steven? If you get up and try to give a message in front of the group you will be displaying a great deal of trust in front of the students, won't you?" He asked me this as we stood outside the centre we were working in which seemed to be in the middle of nowhere in a Swedish wilderness.

There were trees all around us half covered in snow, but no sign of civilisation in this freezing cold air which made your breath turn to steam when you spoke. "I'll think about it." I said to him through steamy breath and from that moment and for the next hour that was all I could think about. "What if nothing happens and I'm left standing there with my mouth open and everyone is looking at me expecting me to get the same kind of messages as Gordon Smith?" I said this out loud to myself in my little room above where the demonstration was to take place. Part of me wanted to do it very much and after all, my teacher was a seasoned medium. Again, I spoke out loud. “He wouldn’t ask me to do this if he didn’t have faith in my abilities, would he?”

The argument went on in my head as I began to dress for the demonstration, even though I was still very uncertain if I would try this, a part of me seemed to carry on dressing in my suit and fixing myself in preparation for my big test. Just then there was a knock on my door and I knew it was Gordon, coming to see if I would get up with him or if I would chicken out. In my head it was the latter, but I was surprised as I opened the door and saw him smile at me. “Good, you’re doing it then, I thought you would.” I wanted to tell him that I could still change my mind, but I didn’t and instead I walked with him downstairs towards the larger room where about forty people had gathered for the demonstration.

Gordon began the night by talking to the audience about how the mediumship might work and that if they did get a message, they should speak back to him or me, whoever

was working. It hit me at this moment that I had passed a point of no return and that now the people were expecting me to get up on my feet in a moment and give messages from the spirit world. My only real memory was that my body was shaking from the inside and I honestly didn't know if people watching me could see this. The word "HELP" went through my head like a mantra over and over until I heard the people clapping their hands as I had just been introduced to the platform to give the first message.
I don't remember what it felt like to stand up, but somehow my body was doing it automatically and to my surprise I was talking and with each word the nerves began to subside and I was pointing to a woman who sat at the back of the room and I could hear my voice telling her that her mother in the spirit world had a message for her and that she was not a Swedish lady but she came from Denmark and she had passed away very recently.

The recipient of the message said yes and no sooner had she answered me when more streams of information flowed out of me. During this process I felt calm and very together, almost safe like someone was holding me. I immediately went on to the next message that was taken by a younger woman sitting near to the front of the crowd; it was her father who was communicating now. Once again, the message came through very easily and a force that was much higher than me was controlling me, it all felt like it was being guided and I was too.

I don't know what really happened after that, because the whole time Gordon got up and gave his messages, I felt numb until the moment it was over; even the messages I gave seemed to fade from my mind into a kind of blur. I wanted to remember everything and talk to my teacher about what had just happened, but he reassured me that it was quite normal for mediums not to remember messages after they had given them. He said this happened because the information wasn't created in the brain of the medium, but was created in the spirit world and only channelled through the medium, so it wasn't always remembered by the medium.

Good, bad or indifferent, I had done it. I got up in front of an audience and given two messages from the other-side and taken the leap of faith, which my teacher asked of me and showed that I was willing to put my trust in spirit to the test. Both people I spoke to came to me later and thanked me for what they said were good messages from loved-ones, though to be honest, it was all still a bit of a mystery to me. It took a few days after our return from the Swedish trip to realise what I had done. I had taken a step forward in my development and it felt right somehow.

Many times before this I had been given chances to grow and I would just shy away from them, but now I had trusted my guide, or my intuition or something deeper than my everyday mind and because of this, I felt something had changed in me. I do believe that I got a little bit of understanding about letting go and taking a leap into the dark for what I believed in. I do think when the opportunity comes in our spiritual development to take that chance that it will be right if you are doing what you truly believe in and also, I trusted my teacher in this world and this was my chance to show him this. All in all, this one little moment in my life showed me that if I trust in my belief and in myself then positive change will follow, and that certainly did happen for me.

During our spiritual development we will all be given chances to trust in the spirit world and if we succeed, then we cannot help but grow. I believe that I will always have the ability to give messages from the other-side, but I honestly know in my heart now that it was my interest in this subject that led me to find my true vocation which is spiritual healing. I have built up such a strong bond with the spirit healers who work through me and show me so many times that positive energy and willing, mixed with good intentions and trust, can change many people for the better.

I think your spiritual practice becomes much stronger when you can tell yourself "I trust in my work." The reason

I can say that now with my hand on my heart is because of all the proof and evidence I have been given by the higher forces I believe in. I think it is important when you arrive at this point, that you honour your guides and thank them for all the good work they have done for you; the more you trust in the spirit, the more you can truly trust your place on the path.

**Exercise 4: Sensing your Path**

This exercise is about trusting your guide and putting a bit of your life in their hands so to speak; it's called, SENSING YOUR TRUE PATH. In this practise, you will sit in the power and allow your guide to reveal to you the nature of the work you are to do for them.

1- *Again, we start by going through the process of going into the silence and through each step we have followed to this point. So, sit with a straight back in a chair and relax your shoulders and take a deep breathe, pulling the air slowly into your body and all the way down to the bottom of your lungs before slowly releasing it through the mouth or nose.*

2- *Be still, as you allow your body to relax into your chair, allowing the chair to take the physical weight of your body.*

3- *Keep breathing deeply to begin with and with each in-breath instruct your body to relax by saying this inwardly until you feel your body is becoming heavier.*

4- *Control your thinking by becoming aware of your thoughts, but don't follow them or attach to them to them – just let them fade in the distance and be aware of making your mind quiet.*

5- *As the body and mind become relaxed and quiet, try to notice the silence in the atmosphere around you and balance your inner self with this outer peace and stillness.*

6- *Sit for a while in this silence but keep control of your quiet mind and don't allow yourself to sleep, but stay in this light altered state of mind.*

7- *Send out a thought from your mind to your spirit guide. Ask that the guide will come into this state of stillness with you and just open up to perceive any sensations that occur in the atmosphere around you. Even as thoughts try to rise in you, again, do not follow them but instead just sit and get used to the feeling of sensing the presence of your guide in your space.*
8- *Sit in this amazing energy, just getting to know the feeling of being close to a highly evolved spiritual being. Resist the temptation to think or try to describe the guide, try to just be in this moment for as long as you can.*
9- *Allow the guide to lift your vibration to their own higher vibration and again, try to resist doing anything, just "TRUST YOUR GUIDE"*
10- *Ask quietly in your mind how you might serve the spirit world and wait. Allow what happens next to just unravel, if nothing happens, it's because you are not ready to know your path at this point, be patient. If you sense that your energy is changing*

*register what is happening to you. If you see pictures, study and remember them that you might work them out at the end, but trust your feelings, spirit speaks to us through our feelings, so learn how to interpret what is happening; again, if you don't know how to, you are not yet ready.*

11- *Thank the guide for being present and ask them to step out of your space and as this happens, begin to breathe air back into your body. With each breath you take, your mind will become more alert and you will feel the weight of the body again. When you feel that you are fully awake, open your eyes and stretch your body.*

Till now I have shared with you some of the early exercises I learned in my development with my teacher. Now I choose to put them together and make one practise which I teach people in the early part of my teaching program. This practise is all about disciplining your mind and trusting your guide. In essence, you are doing a simple meditation, but it is all preparation for more progressive work that will come later in your spiritual practice. In any form of spiritual practise, the practitioner has to trust the higher power and learn to lose all doubts from the mind.

I know that in my early training I had so many questions about this practise, asking if the spirit comes into my body or my mind and how will I know they will have left and so on and how can I trust the information that comes. All of this type of early thinking is quite natural at the beginning, but as you practise regularly you find that the questions become less and the experience gets much richer and less pressured.

I would like all my students to practise this type of session at least once a week at the same time and in the same place if possible and where possible, with other people who want to develop the same kind of spiritual practise as you. The same place and time are really just to become familiar and trusting, the same with the people aspect, but in fact you can do this on your own if you chose to, though some people are a bit reluctant to sit with spirit on their own.

It reminds me of a time when I was in London assisting on a weekend seminar when one of the students pulled me aside, asking me if I could teach her how to trust her guide as she was very scared that the guide might start to want to control her life and she said she was a little uncertain about the idea of spirit guides coming into her space when she was meditating.

I totally understood her reservations as I thought things like this myself before I had proper teaching. It was because I came through the type of experiences I did, that I was well positioned to help this woman. I told her to try to do the exercise we have just done and not try to rush to do anything else; to feel the presence of the guide because when she truly got to sense the guide it would feel loving and nurturing and nothing fearful or threatening at all. She agreed to try this and report back to me in the future.

Several weeks later I heard from her and she was using my exercise with two friends every week and they were all beginning to feel a strong but comforting energy in their little circle. It was great for me to hear this because I knew that this practise is what really helped me to grow spiritually because I learned to trust the guides from the spirit world and not fear them and this is almost exactly what this lady said to me some weeks on from our first meeting.

I think that this simple word, TRUST, is one of the most important you will encounter on your spiritual journey and it won't just appear once or twice, in fact it is on-going and will usually come towards you when you think you have learned a great lesson. I know that I still have a lot to trust and to try on my own pathway, but I also believe that it is how much I have learned to trust in a force from an unseen world that I have risen above many of the issues I had when I first came on to this road. I do believe that I have learned to trust the spirit world in my practices and also in my everyday life, but I am certain that I will be presented with many more opportunities to show just how much I have grown or not. None the less, these days I am much more open to the challenges than ever before as

I have learned that when we experience real trust then something very, very, good will happen. Trust me…

# 7.

## UNIVERSAL HEALING

*Compassion is to healing what coal is to a fire.*

There are so many types of healing practices on offer these days and millions of people all over the world are beginning to look into this sort of alternative medicine for answers to what ills them. To be honest, I tend to stick to working with spirit healing, though I am always interested to hear about and study other forms of healing. Like all things in this field there are those who are very good, some which are mediocre and then those downright nonsensical.

When I began to practice my healing abilities on others, my mind began to wonder about all the many people before me who caused people to get better using no more than healing powers. I think that for the first time in my life I actually looked at the bible and some of the many stories describing miraculous healings. Such as the time when Jesus was said to have cured people who had leprosy, which would have been beyond any cure of the time, or even when he was reported to have raised Lazarus from the dead – could these things really have happened?

Such stories seemed so far back in time and my mind wanted to find answers in more recent times where there might be proofs to back up healer's claims. At the beginning of my search, I was shocked to find just how many people in history, recent and past, believed in the powers of healing. Many of the main religions as well as Christianity also talk of healing energies and practices such as rituals and prayers, not to mention the worship and belief in healing spirits, angels and deities. There are special places in the world where people flock to be healed in pools of healing water and in some cases, offerings are made to saints and avatars in return for wellbeing. Learning about these things helped me to accept that my own abilities didn't seem to be so rare or mystical.

I think that I was beginning to realise that healing has been around the world of man for as long as he can remember and even though to many it may be considered a last option, but none the less, what I was doing didn't appear so bizarre I as had maybe first imagined.
One of the accounts of great healing I came across in my search was related to the Irish medium and healer Albert Best whose amazing abilities totally shocked me. A videotape from the Gibraltar Psychical Research Group had footage of some of the mediums and healers who had been filmed using their gifts while visiting them. The clip featuring Mr Best, who looked quite elderly at the time and also very ordinary, that is until he was led into an adjoining room where a woman and man in their forties were waiting. At this point nothing much was happening, then the camera zoomed in to the woman's neck to show a very large swelling. It looked like she had some sort of growth under her skin and she appeared to be in a distressed state when asked to move her head to let the healer examine her.

I don't know what I expected to see, but what followed just looked like nothing much, as Albert closed his eyes and began to mumble in a whispered voice, words I couldn't make out, in fact it sounded like a foreign language to me. His hands raised and still with his eyes closed and mumbling, he made some passes with his hands around the woman's neck and head. The whole thing could only have lasted for a few minutes at most, when it came to an abrupt end and the healer opened his eyes and spoke normally again, he said something like, "are you OK, Misses?"

The woman just nodded a reply and then her husband exclaimed. "My God it's gone." As the camera again cut to her neck it was clear to see that the large lump was not there anymore; it had completely vanished! As I watched I saw Mr. Best calmly leave the room as if nothing had happened and as if he had no interest in the miraculous happening, leaving the couple hugging and both reduced to tears of joy. To watch something like this has to make you wonder what and how this could actually happen?

Such phenomenal healing leaves you bewildered and makes you think that what you have just witnessed is either staged and a clever set-up, or something very miraculous and unexplainable in normal terms. I chose to think of what I saw on that tape as the latter. The other exceptional thing about this amazing footage is how understated the healer seemed at the end of it. Albert Best looked like it was just so matter of fact as he sauntered out of the healing room, not waiting to take any glory for the incredible thing he had just caused.

Healers like Albert along with others I found astonishing, like Harry Edwards and Nan McKenzie, humbly gave their gift to people who were suffering, feeling that it was an honour to serve the spirit world. If we look at just those three, I have mentioned and not counting so many others who healed to the same high standard, we are still looking at many tens of thousands of people benefiting from the care of spiritual healers. I find myself fortunate to have been taught by Gordon who actually worked alongside Albert Best, like his young understudy and though he never met Harry Edwards or Nan McKenzie, he worked with many people who did and who shared accounts of their miraculous work, which he happily shared with me.

Mrs. Nan McKenzie, who was born in 1882 and practiced her quite phenomenal healing almost to the day she died at the amazing age of one hundred and four in 1986, was someone whose work could only inspire any budding healer. In a book I was given about her life simply titled, Nan McKenzie – Medium and Healer, which was written by Rosalind Cattanach, I was able to read about how this very humble and extremely caring woman caused cures of cancers, tumours, disfigurements and paralysis, along with many other ailments. To read about the extensive cures was something, but if you are looking to further your own abilities of healing from this inspired woman and others like her, I think you also have to look at the character, which to all extents sounds like such people are filled with human kindness and compassion.

The same with Mr. Harry Edwards, a healer whose name became legendary in the Spiritualist world in the 1930's and remained so until his death in 1976. On one astonishing occasion Mr. Edwards was asked to demonstrate his gift before a room of doctors in Harley Street. I might add the patients he worked with were brought there by some of the doctors who obviously knew the history of each patient. Edwards dealt with a woman whose body was paralysed and bent, her back poker-straight with one-foot bent and dragging on the floor. Within the space of only one minute after Edwards moved his hands across the woman's back, she was able to bend forward for the first time in years. It was reported that none of the doctors gave any feedback to the healer at this amazing outcome, but the healer continued and soon the woman could move her legs and feet and eventually stood up under her own steam, this did cause the medical men to react. One of the senior Doctors in the room commented that Harry Edwards had done the work of a surgeon without any operation ever taking place, and also within minutes. It moves me to think that so many people were made whole again because of this gentle man's brilliant gift.

It is wise for all students of healing to look at the past and learn from some of the masters of this craft who put themselves out on a limb for what they believed in. They were true pioneers of an ancient skill, which they fought to bring into a world of more modern thinking.
In my own search for amazing healers, I began to learn that it doesn't matter if the healer is Jesus Christ, or Rasputin who though at times was thought of as a mad monk, yet still brought cure to the son of the Tsar of Russia when called upon. The true element of the healing gift is compassion. I honestly feel that if you care about those you heal, then it truly helps and even adds to the power of healing which channels through you.

The three spiritual healers I mentioned before were all described as very compassionate people by those who knew them. And most of the people I have come across who do what I do, chose this path because they care and because they want to make people better. It would be hard to imagine someone who had great healing abilities who didn't care or show compassion for their patients. In fact, I once heard a tale when I was working in Scotland of a healer who practiced in the Highlands sometime during the last fifty years or so. The story goes, that this man had brought cure to hundreds of the local people around where he lived and that he was known for miles to many highland people as a truly natural healer until one night when he was told that a man in a neighbouring village who he apparently had fallen out with had been taken ill and was asking if the healer would come to his aid. It was said that the healer refused to tend to the patient and even though he spoke to the messenger saying he knew that he was going against his gut feelings, he completely refused to help. Apparently, from that moment until his death his healing abilities completely left him and he was never able to bring cure to anyone again.

I don't know if this story is true, but it definitely makes me think that to be a healer and not have compassion for another's suffering, no matter who, would make your gift quite contradictory and must bring questions to the mind of the healer. As I mentioned earlier, I believe that all the true healers I have seen and worked with are caring people because the work demands that of you, but I felt that it was right to mention the demise of the highland healer, maybe just to remind people that gifts can be given and taken away if misused when we know that the true power is higher than us?

Another person who fascinated my mind when I looked at healers from the past was the Italian monk called Padre Pio. There is much written about this very humble, yet extraordinary man and his amazing powers, but then one part of his extensive healing power that touched me most was his ability to heal people who were thought of as beyond help. In one account I came across it is said that in 1947 a young blind girl who it was said had been born without pupils in her eyes, was taken to the Padre by her grandmother in the hope that he might do prayers for the child, but during the session the teenager reported being able to see images and shortly after this learned to see!

This amazing healer was also reported to be able to heal people who were far away from him by projecting his spirit to where they were; again, I found this type of healing fascinating. Some years before I read about Padre Pio, I had several experiences where I felt myself heal people from distance, so to find that there were actual written testimonies of a very recognised healer who practised what I knew as "Absent Healing," (something we will look at later in the book) this just added to my now strong belief in the powers of love and compassion and that such elements of healing know no bounds within time or space.

**Exercise 5: Self-Healing**

Before I was ever allowed to practise healing on patients my teachers, advised me to do this next exercise, which involved healing myself. It is important for healers to keep themselves in a good state of balance, especially because they will work with people who are out of sorts. This I find also helps me emotionally; it is now part of my weekly practise, so healers – heal thy self.

*We take ourselves through the usual practice, stilling and quietening the mind to the point where we feel ready to welcome our guide into our sacred space. Sit like this and allow the connection between you and your guide to become strong and recognisable.*
*When you have felt the code of recognition, or calling card, which you normally sense when the guide comes, then be comfortable and relax into this moment and enjoy sitting in the presence of your guide.*
*From the quiet of your mind, ask the guide if you may have some healing and then be still and observe the process of healing if it happens. There are times when the spirit does not respond because there is no need for you to be healed at that moment.*

*When then healing begins, try to sense if there is any change in the energy you are sitting in. Is there any change to the temperature, either it is getting hotter, or cooler.*
*If pictures come into your mind, register them without following your thoughts or inventing them. There might be*

*significance in the symbology of the pictures, which can give answers to mental or emotional problems later when you investigate or analyse them.*
*Relax and enjoy the experience of allowing the spirit to heal you, body or mind, present or past, be still and learn to accept the healing energy, knowing that if the healer can find balance through the energies, they can do the same for their patients.*

*There will come a point when you will feel a change in the energy and the intensity will fade, this is the moment to thank your guide and bring an end to the practice.*
*Come back in the usual way until you feel quite alert and awake and grounded. Now is the time to go over what just happened and look at any experiences you just had. It is often wise when there have been picture images given during you meditation to make notes and date them, especially if you are uncertain what they mean at the time. Actually, it is always good to do this at the end of any spiritual session you have.*

The practice of self-healing is something I recommend that students who have reached this level of development should practice at least once a week. Not only do we benefit from the healing energies, but form this exercise we can truly form a much stronger bond with our guide during such sessions and learn more about self and our own requirements.

# 8.

# HEALING IN CIRCLE

*Many people spend their life trying so hard to be individual, yet only when they become part of a group do they truly see themselves in the eyes of others.*

I have mentioned our circle so many times to this point without really touching on the true importance of its effect on my progression and development into healing. Though it started with just the three of us, in time we ended up with seven people sitting regularly each week in Jim and Gordon's home which was now no longer in London, but in Hertfordshire, so that meant a two-hour journey for me each time. The journey meant nothing to me because it was one of those things that excited me at the time, being able to sit with my friends in a private circle where we could all relax and meditate and create a link with our spirit friends.

The circle is like the spiritual classroom in many ways; it is where the student can relax and let go more knowing all the while that the leader is in total control of everything that is occurring within the group. Gordon was our circle leader and he had been sitting in circle for more than twenty years at that time. He was very experienced and was able to help guide us through our meditations and also assist us in mapping out the different mental and emotional states that we might encounter when we practiced.

Though during the early years of my development in this group, much of what I learned was about me and my own mind journey; it was about helping me to create a stronger, clearer mind in preparation to build a stronger, truer link to the spirit who would work with me. Now, as the group got bigger, the work we were doing was more in keeping with spiritual healing and as a group it felt like we were able to do more as the collective mind of the group felt much more powerful.

In one of the sessions we did, Gordon asked us if we could all concentrate our energies on his friend who was pregnant at the time. This lady was quite ill during the early part of her pregnancy and it was feared that she might lose her child. She had called Gordon and asked if he could find a reputable healer for her as she lived in Scotland and knew that he could not get to her in person, so instead of searching for a healer in her area he told her that his circle would do distant healing for her and that is what we did.

I remember how strange it felt when during the early part of the circle where we would sit in the silence and quieten our minds, that it was hard not to want to focus on the task of sending healing after we had been told, but so many sessions of disciplining the mind had taught me not to try and so I became quiet and still. I felt the calling card of my guide as I was now quite used to this and nothing in or around me stirred as my mind relaxed even further until my breath was all that was active in me and I was

aware of just sitting in the presence and highly charged energy of my guide.
I was ready to send out a thought to the spirit to mention the name of the woman we were dedicating the energy to, when I realised that they must already know this and I remained in my silent state, trusting that the right thing would be done, when suddenly I had a mental vision of a woman being carried into an ambulance, she was short and had short dark hair and the feeling that accompanied the vision was one of panic, but I knew this was not my panic so in my quiet mind I just observed and trusted that what we were all doing now would help in some way. At the end of the session, others in the group had experienced similar episodes to mine; some described the scene a little differently from me, yet the theme was almost identical, in that there was an ambulance and a sense of panic followed by calm and none of us picked up any bad feeling to follow.

It wasn't until the following week at the beginning of the next circle that we learned that the lady was taken to hospital that night and that she was threatened by a miscarriage, but she explained later in a phone call, how she suddenly felt a calm wash over her as she got into the ambulance and all her fear subsided and was replaced by a sense of letting go and surrender; it was then that her bleeding stopped and by the time she reached the hospital she felt OK. After being in hospital for only one night she was released and told to be very careful, but her pregnancy continued and happily to her full term when she was able to celebrate the birth of a healthy baby girl. I found it incredible that her scare came at the very time we were sitting as a circle sending her healing. It was equally as strange that everyone in the circle picked up the ambulance and the panic followed by a sense of peace. I also wonder if the spirit world put all of these things in motion while somehow already knowing the outcome long before we did? I felt this as I recalled the moment in circle where I nearly shared the woman's name with my guide but trusted instead that spirit was already aware. If this were so, then wouldn't it be logical to believe Spirit also knew all of the circumstances... and that being the case, I also wondered why we were involved at all, if spirit could do it without us!

The answer to this question came to me when I sat in our next session, after being told the outcome. Spirit wanted us to be part of this episode as a group, knowing that if we put our minds and good intentions together as a one united force that it would have a positive effect, not only for the woman and baby, but also for us. Our trust in the spirit world would be given a boost and a lesson would be shown to us of how strong our healing can be when we truly unite in compassionate efforts to help others. During our times in the Hertfordshire circle, we were asked by many different people for spiritual assistance and healing and always when we concentrated our force for others, so many good things happened in response. For me it felt so different from the individual development. Though both are necessary; it was the circle work that always brought me more satisfaction. I must also point out that even when you are working as a group, each individual is still learning and growing spiritually in their own space too.

It wasn't only healing that was happening in our circle at that time. One of the most important aspects of my development circle was learning about altered states of consciousness, or trance. It was something that was happening to me more and more during our sessions; I would find myself going deeper into my mind and losing the need to stay connected to the room we were sitting in. For mediums and healers to be able to let go more and sink into the deeper parts of their mind means that they are happy to give more control to the spirit who works with them. When this state reaches a certain point the sense of spirit is quite tangible and becomes more detectable in the atmosphere around you and in the circle itself. If all the sitters can tune in to the same deep state, or frequency, then all will be able to sense the same spirit beings and on many occasions we all did, so when this happens everyone is able to describe almost identically what the others experienced and so on.

In essence, the circle is creating a condition, which allows the spirit and the sitter to meet halfway if you like. This happens because we are letting go of our usual upper mind and physical reality and becoming more attuned and focussed on our spiritual, or light self, which means that energies of a spiritual nature are more real for that time than those, which are physical.

I know that many people think that when a medium is in a trance that they have no idea what is happening to them, but this isn't true. The trance states that mediums and some healers experience is a more like an overshadowing which means that even though you can quieten your mind and link with your spirit guide, there are variables of the amount of your being the guide requires. E.g. a clairvoyant medium only has to open up the visual part of their mind to see images given by the spirit guide. In such a case the images enter the medium's mind just like ordinary thoughts, which means that the medium would not have to be in a deep trance to do such a thing, whereas a medium who works with clairsentience where they sense the presence of spirit and what they felt like, might have to give a little bit more of themselves, but still don't have to go deep into a trance. It is more likely that the spirit guide will only have to use more of the medium's mind and functions if they wanted to speak directly to someone or in healing, take control of the body functions and guide the healer's movements or even speech if it should be required.

In the earlier healing I described, when Mr Albert Best was seen to remove a lump from a woman's neck, this was done while the healer was in an altered state of consciousness. During this procedure Albert's guide who was a Chinese Doctor was controlling his mind and body for the short time it took to carry out the procedure; at the very moment it was over, Albert was back as Albert. I learned that Albert always said he was never in a deep state of sleep-like trance during these sessions, he described it more like being in a daydream, in so much that his mind was always slightly aware of where he was and what was happening, but he had no interest in connecting with it, like a daydream as he says.

I have experienced this type of overshadowing or trance healing and when I sense that my mind is going down into a still, quiet state, I just allow it to be, as I know then that my guide for some reason requires me to be less present during the healing session. It used to be that I wanted to always be aware and always ask questions of my guide during healing, but now I believe that I am growing a bit more as I tend now to trust the process and the spirit and when I can do this the results always appear to be much better.

I have met and I know of many healers who don't sit in circles and who are exceptional in their practice, but I believe that it benefits everyone on a spiritual development path to be part of a strong circle or spiritual group if they can. There is something about having the support of others during your development which seems to help you to progress, not to mention the benefit of being able to share your experiences with other like-minded people that truly helps you to grow. We often found ~~that~~ our circle was used in a healing capacity and not only for people at a distance, often we would get healing as a group or many times one or more individual would feel the energy built that night among the group would be concentrated on them. Now when I teach my own students, I do encourage them to start groups if they can and I usually find those who do, grow in body mind and spirit.

**Exercise 6: Group Healing and Absent Healing in Circle**

This practice can be done as an individual or as part of a group or circle and for this exercise I will guide to the individual and explain at the end how it would change for the spiritual circle or group of healers.

Begin as always by relaxing your body and quieting the mind and take yourself *into the silence.*

*From the quiet of your mind send out a thought of welcome to your guide and wait until you feel their code or calling card.*

*Be still and sit in the presence of your guide and allow the connection between you to strengthen.*

*When you feel that the bond between you has been formed, visualise the person or situation you want to heal. Ask the guide to help you to heal while you hold the visual in your mind. Register any sensations and feelings in your space; especially if you feel extreme difference in temperature, or feeling of vibration around you. This type of change can often signify that healing is strong and functioning. As with the exercise in self-healing, be aware of any pictures or symbols that might appear in your mind while you are concentrating on the healing energy, such images might be instructive about the situation you are trying to heal.*

*As before, allow the energy to fade before asking the guide to step out of your space and bring your mind back to a state of alertness back in the room. For groups to carry out the same procedure, I always feel that it is good to begin by joining hands and creating a physical bond between the sitters until the point where the group is sitting in the silence. On many occasions our group would feel the power building up like a warm wave of energy flowing around the circle. If all sitters are told to visualise the patient or situation being healed in the centre of the circle there seems to be a much stronger force to the exercise. Always in such groups, it is amazing how synchronised the effort, experiences and timing of the people; it often feels like each person can have almost identical occurrences during the session.*

The practice of a circle doing absent or distant healing is quite similar to sending prayers en masse, though in the case of healing the practice is made stronger by the intensity of feeling over just thought, though both can have amazing effect on the recipients, either way, it's worth it to the recipient if it works.

# 9.

# LETTING GO

*It's not wise to dabble in the unknown; it's certainly a lot better to immerse yourself in it.*

Seven years of my development had passed and I found myself in a similar position to the one I was in back in Frankfurt several years before. I was stepping out in front of a group of students, only now I was on my own with no one beside me. For the first time I would be taking a workshop without the help of my teacher. I had been part of so many of those trips and met thousands of students over the years, some of who became firm friends, but till now I had always been seen as my teacher's right-hand man. How different it would feel to stand in front of a group on my own and with only my trust in the spirit teachers who had worked through me and guided me from the other world, physically I would be standing alone.

It all happened during one of the many trips Gordon and I made to Basel. I was standing talking to a group of students during one of the breaks when a woman approached me asking if I would consider taking a workshop on my own, but teaching the same exercises that were being taught on this course. I honestly felt flattered but till that moment had never thought about teaching classes on development away from my teacher. I must admit it made me feel a little perplexed and a shade uneasy at first.
When I spoke to Gordon about the woman's suggestion, he seemed less bothered about the idea of me working on my own and actually encouraged me saying. "It's about time you moved on." The very sound of his words made me think I was leaving something which had become very familiar, like when you first leave home, or move up from low school to high school; it all felt very weird, but

something inside of me was stirring and I knew that it all felt organic and totally natural.

I know I said it was a bit like being back in Frankfurt, but it actually wasn't because now I had so much experience under my belt and talking to people in public about a subject I had come to know was really not so scary anymore. I so enjoyed my first teaching session, it was held in the Austrian Alps and there was a group of some thirty odd people who came to take part in what was to be a four-weekend workshop, which would run over the course of a year.   It was during this time that I was asked to give healing to a young man who had a very intense condition of epilepsy. His name was Matias and he was 22 years old and he came to me accompanied by his mother who was really at her wits end because of the number of seizures her poor son was experiencing. She explained to me that he would fit almost twenty times a day, every day. She was determined to try to get her boy to anyone who might be able to help him no matter what.  I remember that during the first session of healing with Matias how deep the connection was between me and my guide, there was a moment when I even felt that my hands where not mine anymore, but actually overshadowed by someone else's. There was a real deep feeling of the spirit being in total control of this exercise and Matias just seemed to fall asleep as my hands simply passed over his head and shoulders. I can't really remember thinking during this process, I can honestly say that my thinking mind had been turned down so low that I was aware, but I had no real interest. For me it felt like I had completely let go and trusted that my guide would know what to do for this young man.

At the end of the session, I spoke softly to my young client, encouraging him to come back from his nap. I asked him how he was and he didn't speak, but nodded slowly, still trying to regain full consciousness again. I didn't expect anything to happen immediately, but I would never rule that out, especially when spirit works in such a close manner, but either way I would never promise anything by way of hope. It is my way to let the healing speak for itself and if any change was to come, we would all know soon enough. Several months had passed before I travelled to Austria again and when I did, I scheduled another session of healing for Matias, as his mother had requested this, plus I wanted to hear if there had been any progression after the first session. His mother excitedly headed straight towards me when she caught sight of me standing in the little community hall where I had been teaching my workshop earlier that day. "Steven, I really cannot thank you enough." I knew by this that there must be positive news concerning her son and there was. Though Matias was still having seizures, he was now only experiencing them once or twice a week compared with the daily nightmare from before and his mother told me that during the fits, his reaction was less severe than before. I was so pleased because to see someone so young in his life being held back from what so many would call a normal life because of illness was horrible. When I saw him walk into the room a moment after his mother, I noticed that even the way he walked looked more positive, like there was more of a spring in his step and he had a look in his eyes that he couldn't wait to get started with the next session.

Matias's healing is one that I remind myself of if ever in a very rare moment of my life when I would ever doubt the power and good work of the spirit world. Shortly after our second session I received a letter from his mother informing me that his fits had now all but stopped and that he was getting his life back. This lady was so overcome by what happened and so grateful to me, but I had to remind her that it is the spirit world who channel through me who do the work and that I am really just the vessel.

It doesn't really bother me to believe that I am only the instrument because I know that what I feel during these sessions when the spirit use me to help others, that I benefit from the experience as every time I sense the love and amazing energy of my guide in the spirit world and that is something which is often beyond words.

The course which I taught in Austria was also received very well with all the students asking if I could come back and take another the following year, which was so good for my

confidence, remember, that was the first time I had done this without being under the watchful eye of my teacher. I believe that after my Austrian trip that something changed in me. I did feel more confident in my work and also in the spirit world; it really felt that something had shifted again and for me – that felt good. It was a sort of buzz to realise that I could do this on my
own, it showed me how far I had come in my personal development and though I still assist my teacher during some seminars and workshops teaching people about spiritual development, many more times now I am asked to come and conduct some on my own, which I do with no fuss or fear.

I do believe that the more I grow, the more I know about my work and about the spirit who work with me. At the outset of my development back in Pimlico, Gordon told me that all the things, which I didn't understand at the time would become clear to me, but he said that no answers he gave me then would make sense because the answers only come when a person is ready to understand them. Now, I totally know what he meant and though I am aware that I still have a way to go, it is nice to be able to say that I understand the direction I am headed on.

There is most definitely a theme through the process of development and for me that would stand out as, "LETTING GO." I don't believe that any teacher can teach you this, I know mine, pointed me towards the moments where I would be tested and asked to let go and take those leaps of faith that change our life, but no one but me could actually make the step that would define the new direction that would follow. Having spoken with many others who have been on the road to development, those who make such leaps all say the same thing and that they all felt a massive shift for the better after a test, which was scary and unthinkable.
Gordon once told me that every time he uses his mediumship for the public it is like make a leap of faith because no matter how many times he has done this, each time still feels like the first time because each time there is a group of new people with new losses and individual needs. I feel similar with healing when I offer to help

someone that nothing I have done before will matter to the new patient and only what comes from the session will be relevant or important to them. Regardless of all this, it is a privilege to heal people and be a channel for spirit energy. It is an amazing thing to see hope come back into peoples' eyes because of what you have done and it is its own reward to have any spiritual experience, which is why I love to use my gift when I can.

**Exercise 7: One Way of Healing**

For students whom are ready to use the healing practise on others I offer this system of healing taught to me by my teachers. Please remember though, at the outset, you are a student and therefore it is best to try this on others who sit in circle with you or on your friends and family, I found that when I did this my confidence grew in my work.

*Always begin by making your patient feel comfortable. Make sure they are sitting comfortably and allow them to speak to you about their condition. Explain to your patient how the healing will work, e.g. If you begin by taking their hands or any other sort of physical touch, make sure your patient is comfortable with this procedure, be clear about how you work and describe it as best you can before you begin.*

*I always start by standing behind my seated patient, gently resting my hands on their shoulders until I feel the patient relax. During this time I open my mind and ask for my guide to be present and allow myself to be used as a channel. When you feel the presence of the spirit allow them and their force to lift your hands up from the physical body and be guided by spirit. If you totally trust, the spirit will guide your hands around the patient without touching them physically. Be open to what is happening, but let go of controlling thoughts, if your own thoughts come in just be aware that you are thinking but do not connect with them.*

*Your body may sense what the patient is feeling at this time, such empathy comes with healing and if it does, just allow it but again don't become fixed on it. When you feel that the session is coming to a close, thank your guide and allow them to step out of your space.*

*I rest my hands again gently on the patient's shoulders, letting them know that the session is at a close, this is something I have told them before I begun. Move to the front of your patient as they come back and ask them to tell you what they experienced during the healing, some of what they say, you may have picked up and it is better not to tell the patient what you experienced until they have expressed their feeling etc.*

*If you feel that you have anything to pass that is helpful or of benefit to their condition then be clear and share exactly what you sensed or picked up. But, give no diagnosis, or pseudo-medical advice.*

*When the patient has left, take a few moments to clear your mind and bring balance to your own mind and energies.*

# 10.

# SELF HEALING

*Healing the self is a daily practice, so healer heal thy self!*

I've shared much about how spiritual healing can have good effect on people who are ailing, but I feel that I must mention that one of the most effective healings I ever did was on myself. One of the reasons I chose to share my healing practices and exercises with the reader was to help them to understand the nature of healing and if a healer can help others, surely, he can help himself – or not?

I began my journey as an ordinary guy with all the same hang-ups and hurdles in my life as most people have; now I find it much easier to handle such problems because of the spiritual practices I underwent in my development. So many people suffer from inner stress related problems, which if left to grow can become illnesses and I find myself more and more these days working with people who have low self-esteem and who feel tired but cannot locate the cause. I am by no means a medical man or a psychologist but it has become quite clear to me that many people put themselves under great amounts of pressure by the way they think about their life. I have encountered so many cases where people feel ill but the medical profession have no answers or indeed cures because the main symptom is born out of worry or concern and negative thinking.

Before I started on my own course of spiritual practice, I was a great worrier. I don't think a day went by when I didn't disrupt my thinking with doubts and negative thoughts. It could be something so simple, like my mother telling me that she had to go to see a doctor for some minor thing and I would start to concern myself and make the situation much worse in my head to the point that fear and dread would consume me; only when I was reassured that she was fine would I let up with my inner concerns.

Worry, I have learned is the fuel for stress and stress becomes a monster that devours the inner self.
During my early meditations with Gordon, he talked to me a lot about stress and how to alleviate it from the self. I don't think I truly understood that at first but as I began to grow as a person, I realised the importance of fixing my own stress and fear. A big part of the development process that I was taught was about how to heal myself and make myself a clear channel and without realising it, I was healing my mind and in so doing I was healing my body and my life for that matter; a strong mind keeps fear at bay.
I devote a big part of my time when I am teaching others about healing to spend time healing themselves because I know how it helps as I myself benefitted from the simple practice of self-healing. People internalise so much that it seems natural to take a little time each week to release the inner pressures we create in our mind.

I believe that this was really brought home to me when I was asked to treat a patient who was deeply depressed and who had become a recluse, not even going out to the local shops or doing the everyday things we all take for granted. This was a woman in her late forties whose family had grown up and whose husband had left her. She was, by her own admission a very lonely person. Her doctor told her she was suffering from depression and offered medication which she refused to take and so she sunk ever deeper into her own sadness. I think when I first visited her that I wanted to give her a good shake as it seemed very clear that she was just wasting her life, but the healer in me felt something else. I remember on the first occasion that she told me that she didn't think that the healing would have any effect on her because nothing could cure her inner hurt and sadness, I wasn't really sure how to proceed, but I did in spite of the wall of negativity she put up.

Healing is an unseen force, which can penetrate many barriers and I know that people do not have to believe in it to get better so I persisted and my thinking was that I would try in spite of the lady's doubt. It was one of those

situations where you just go through the motions of something you have done so many times and even at the end of the session I wondered if it was worth the effort, but I noticed that this woman was in a deep sleep and I just sat myself down on a seat across from her and watched her for a moment until she began to stir. She shook her head from side to side and then said.
"Goodness I must have drifted off for a moment." It was clear that she didn't expect such an effect and everything about her looked brighter than before.
The upshot of this account is that this same woman had several sessions of healing from me before I learned that the best course of action I could offer her was to teach her how to heal herself. Because each time she was going into a sort of meditative state, my intuition told me that she was in fact finding herself in a state of mind that wasn't filled with fear or concern, she was completely still and at peace, the same way I felt when I did my meditation practice.

So, I offered to teach her the simple practice of sitting in the silence by herself and I told her to call upon her own healers to come and help her, as I further explained that we all have healers with us and they were there to help us to bring balance and peace to our mind. In essence, the self-healing is a meditation practice, which allows us to concentrate our efforts on calming both body and mind, which in its self, allows our own healing energy to raise within us. Such a happening allows the spirit around us to add to that energy and the session can often bring about a genuinely beneficial effect.
This particular woman, like many others I have worked with who have similar conditions, did begin to change her attitude and eventually realise that she had to make an effort and be responsible for her life. I believe that any effort people make to make themselves better has got to be better than doing nothing and resigning yourself to giving up on life.

For the students on the spiritual path, the self-healing practice should be part of their course. From my own experience the mind can be strengthened when we feel we have some control of it. I know many who practice affirmations and positive self-help mantras, all of these things can help a person to feel more in charge of their life and destiny.

**Exercise 8: A Way of Self-Healing**

*The exercise is simple and begins by sitting comfortably - the same preparation for sitting in the silence.*

*Relaxing the body and stilling the mind until your breath is the most prominent focus of your awareness.*

*Sit like this for a while and experience the benefit of the quiet mind and be aware of how the breath begins to naturally slow to a pace that brings you to a point of inner stillness.*

*Reach out with your mind to the empty space around you and sense any vibration or rhythm in the atmosphere around your sill body.*

*Now send out a thought to your guide and simply ask for healing for the self. Be aware of any feeling in or around the body but don't react just accept that the energy around you is working for you, to benefit whatever need you have in either body or mind.*

*Allow the session to continue and be aware of any moment when memories come into your thinking mind – register these, but do not add to them, simply let them pass through your mind.*

*Recognise that in this perfectly quiet state you are open to be healed and balanced.*

*As the strength of the energy subsides, start to breathe deeper and with each breath, start to be more aware of the body – filling your lungs with air will bring the brain to a more awakened state.*

*When you are ready you can open your eyes and stretch your arms out and stand up when you feel totally conscious and move the body, shake out the arms and rotate the shoulders.*

*Thank yourself and the spirit for the healing.*

This type of self-healing session can be done whenever you feel you require it. You can also do this in your circle as an individual or as a whole group. I always try to send out all the energy from the group to others who are in need at the end of the session; you can do this yourself also.

## 11.

## ABSENT AND HANDS-ON HEALING

*Some see the space between Heaven and Earth as empty, I see it completely full, full of life, love and possibilities.*

The first true experience I had of absent healing is when I was told that my sister's husband had become very poorly after contracting some viral infection. I was in the second year of my training in Pimlico, in fact, it was around the time when I was being taught how to just sit in the power and feel the presence of my guide, which I remember was becoming quite strong then.

Sitting in my bedroom in my parent's home I decided to do some healing prayers to my brother-in-law and ask my spirit guide to help both he and my sister, who had sounded quite distressed when she told me about her husband on the phone earlier. I think it was because of how upset she sounded that I felt a strong urge to try to help.

I went through the process that I knew from my circle, which was to relax, go into the silence and then open up my space to my guide when almost at once I sensed the same familiar calling card and I knew that something was happening. I recall that the experience was quite vibrant and it seemed like there was a vibrating sensation all around my body, like my Aura was pulsing rapidly.

Concentrating on the image of Dan, my brother-in-law, I somehow felt like I was for a moment standing in front of him in his house. In this moment I experienced no sense of travel, but in the second or so that it took to visualise his face, I felt that I was actually looking at him. What followed this became even stranger. It had been some time since I had visited my sister's home, but I remember distinctly that their sofa was on the wall nearest the door, only in this moment I saw Dan, lying on the sofa which was now against the opposite wall and because of the nature of his business, I had only ever seen him very clean-shaven, yet now he looked to have a very heavy growth of hair around his chin.

I had a strong sense of warmth coming from where I was standing, moving towards Dan. I knew that healing energy was being passed to him and although it was a very bizarre experience, I somehow went along with it until I felt the energy dissolve and I was more aware of being in my bedroom and was very present of the energy of spirit recede, until I was taking deep breaths and making myself much more alert.

I wondered if what happened to me was an out-of-body experience. I had heard of this type of phenomena, but never thought it would happen to me, but then my mind told me that I might have made everything up – remember, this was back at the beginning when my mind was full of questions about my spiritual journey. It wasn't until an hour or so that my sister Kelly called me and asked if I had done some strange psychic thing because she swore that she saw me for a second, standing in her front room. Without hesitation I asked her if they had moved their sofa to the opposite wall and she said they had and I could tell she was wondering what was coming next.

I asked her if Dan had not shaved for several days and did he have a very heavy growth. Again, my sister agreed and I was wondering how to tell her that I had somehow travelled spiritually and found myself in her home when she totally took me unawares by saying. "Steve, I saw you standing in front of Dan about an hour ago and though it was just for a second, I am sure of what I saw." She described the exact clothes I was wearing and this time it was my time to confirm things. The whole thing was quite out there if I say so myself, but my brother-in-law began to recover from that moment on and I suppose that the healing I was asking for got done, though I never expected to some weird psychic house call.

Much of what has happened to me in my spiritual practices has been quite natural and in many ways, intuitive even though I have been through a proper course of development. It is the development, which helps us to understand some of the random phenomena like I have just described. I say this because I really don't think I could teach someone to do this, but it is the type of unprompted things which may occur when you are opening up to the spirit world. Learning under the guidance of a proper teacher helps us not to fear such happenings, instead it helps us to understand them.

Not every attempt at absent healing will end up with you feeling that you are travelling to your patient, in fact most occasions it will be more like distant thinking, where your imagination will conjure a vision for you to concentrate your healing energy on. However, the more I experience spiritual happenings, the more I realise that the spirit around us has many more wonders for me to experience, some from afar and some very close-up and personal.

During my time spent with Jim, he would give me instructions on the practice of healing people, this was something he had great experience in. Jim had in his early teens been part of a charismatic group of spiritual healers in the Catholic Church in Scotland. During his time there he was taught how to do hands-on healing or the laying on of hands. As suggested, it is when the healer physically lays his or her hands on the client's body that effects healing. In Jim's group he told me that this practice was accompanied by calling on the Holy Spirit whose energy would be channelled through the healer into the patient, in much the same way as Spiritualist healers are in essence asking the spirit guide or healing spirit to use their body as a channel.

Jim also ran the healing group in the Glasgow Spiritualist Church for a time and this group followed the SNU (*Spiritualist National Union*) teachings of healing which was more of a non-physical healing and I suppose more in line with the way my own healing developed. There are many healing organisations today, like the *National Federation of Healers* and *Healing Trust* etc. It doesn't do any harm to look at all of the healing arts and always accept what fits with you and feel free to disregard stuff that you don't connect with.

Jim felt that he wanted me to learn something of all the various types of healing on offer. He also gave me books to read on the people who most inspired me like Padre Pio and Harry Edwards and many others. All of this was a great foundation for what was to follow in my development.
I can never thank Jim enough for all he taught me about the arts of healing and also the standard rules and regulations about when it is right to physically connect with a patient and the protocol you would use in such cases. He said that nowadays things have changed so much with healing that something like the laying on of hands would be quite frowned upon by some organisations because of accusations which could be made against a healer in this type of situation (like sensual interaction).

I now inform all my students of the do's and don'ts regarding the practice of healing on clients. I think it is wise to look through some of these, as many people are very confused about the rights and wrongs of spiritual healing. One of the things I always insist of my students is that you must always consult with your patient before the practice and offer them an outline of how the healing will be carried out. I ask every patient before I begin whether or not it is ok that I begin the healing by placing my hands on their shoulders. I then tell them that after this first touch my hands will not make any more physical contact until the end of the session, when, with their permission, I will gently bring my hands to rest where they first began, back on the patient's shoulders.   Most people understand that it is very wrong to lay your hands all over a patient's body, but there are some who insist on doing this. As I have outlined before, healing can be done from a distance, so there is no real need to touch someone. Even in my own practice, if a patient said they didn't want me to start and end with my hands on their shoulders that would be fine, I simply wouldn't do it.

The reason I follow this procedure is firstly because that is how I was taught and also it lets me get a sense of the person at the beginning and it informs the patients that it's over without me having to speak out loud. Many patients drift into light sleep during healing so it's less intrusive. For me it is sometimes with the first touch when I get a strong sense of what is wrong with the person, or in some cases I sense something beneath the surface and for many of the patients the sense of that light touch can be very reassuring and helps them to relax.

Healers must not diagnose illness if they have no medical knowledge or are trained and also licensed to do so, please leave this to the medical profession who have many years of training behind them. Healers must never give false hope to a client or their family out of sympathy. Remember, healers work with compassion, not sympathy and sometimes compassion is tough, it would be so wrong to tell a patient or their family a lie because you are moved by their sadness. If that happens, then it is your sadness that stands out more than the patient's. Just as you mustn't give false predictions of hope, you must never, ever tell a client's family that they will die! Some might be shocked that I would even suggest that this happens, but it has and it is appalling and very upsetting.

It is also so important for healers not to contradict a patient's medical doctor if they are receiving attention from both doctor and healer, both practices should complement one another.

It is important for you to know that when people visit a healer, they do so with a need to feel better, they should never leave you feeling worse, even if nothing happens by way of healing in the spiritual sense, you should be able to refrain from making patients leave feeling worse.
This reminds me of when I was at the Arthur Findlay College when one of the older women who was on our course who told me and my friend that she was a healer. She offered to do healing on my friend who at the time had a bad back and felt that this offer was quite coincidental as we had been talking about how to find out how you could get healing on the course. I must point out that this woman was not one of the SNU registered healers and she took my friend off to her room to give him some healing. It was when he returned that I noticed ~~that~~ he looked much worse than when he first went off with

her. He said that she banged on his back with her fist and said that her guide was a bit heavy handed, he was a Viking apparently, the physical beating was bad enough, but she really shook him when she said that he had an illness that she could feel was about to come to the fore and that he should visit a doctor when he got home. Can you imagine what that kind of information does to a person's mind not to mention their wellbeing?

Over the course of the night, we told other students what happened and not many were surprised, as some of them had also encountered the bashing Viking healer and all had been beaten to a pulp and then given a deathly prediction about their health. OK, we were able to laugh at this episode, but what if that were told to someone who was very worried about their health, or someone who was a bit unstable. Honestly, this is why you should always know that your healer is someone you know you can trust and respect and I think you will be able to tell that if they treat you with the same trust and respect.

# 12.

# HEALING THROUGHOUT THE TIMES

"Not everything in life will change, compassion is forever"

Healing has changed over the years because the world has changed and people now have access to many more spiritual practices, not to mention information on healing and other spiritual gifts. For me, Healing has become a big part of my everyday life and I strive to make people more aware of the benefits of this old, yet new art.
I feel that I have moved on from the days of sitting round the pub with my mates talking football and girls to sitting around seminars all over Europe talking about philosophy and spiritual phenomena; some change yeah? Not only this, I now run my own private circle in London and have started to teach classes in development at the very special London Spiritual Mission in Notting Hill Gate in West London. This is where Mrs Nan Mackenzie and Albert Best

and other great healers and mediums shared their amazing spiritual gifts.

There have been so many people over the years who miraculously have been able to cure the sick in many different and some in very obscure ways, with lotions and potions, prayers and incantations and even channelling. And then there are those who have just used the laying on of hands. I don't think it matters when the cure of the ailment is produced to the betterment of the suffering. I do however feel that times and people are changing and therefore we have to be careful and respect those we work with, always taking care to be sensible and mindful of their needs.  Spiritual healing is an amazing gift if managed properly, if given to those who deserve it in time of suffering and need. To all practitioners of the art of healing I say. "More than one person will benefit from a healing if the patient's need is true and the channel is open."

At this point I would like to offer my healing prayer to all the readers of this book. Before I started out in my own

journey in my early twenties, I don't think I even thought about sending out prayers to others, not because I was selfish, but more for the fact that it just never occurred to me that my good intentions could cause any effect on another person.
Since I first began to practice as a healer, I have learned that taking a few moments of my time to dedicate my thoughts and prayers to people or situations in need, certainly can help. For all those who are interested in developing as a healer I say, "a strong prayer life can benefit the healer along with the recipient of their prayer."
Prayer can be done anywhere or at any time, that's what makes it so easy. I always direct my prayers through my spirit guide, but most others would focus on God, or saints etc. It really doesn't matter if your intentions are true.

*"Gracious Spirit, please can you help this person... I ask that you might use my energy if it is necessary to lift their spirit and allow them to find true balance in their life once again. I also ask that this prayer might reach out to all who are affected by this situation and hope that they also might find peace once again.*

*I trust that you will do all that can be done at this time, but you will continue to send love and compassion from the spirit world.*
*Thank you gracious spirit for hearing me.*

Remember, a true prayer only needs to be said once from the heart, it shows that you trust those you put your faith in.
I hope with all my heart that those who read this book will benefit from the stories and practices I have laid out for you. In the course of my short and humble journey into the world of healing I have felt blessed to be guided by my teachers in both worlds and more than this, to be able to help others. Therefore, if this book helps you in some small way, then my work is continuing.

Best Wishes,
Steven Levett

# 13.

## Frequently Asked Questions

Those have no questions need no answers, is that you?"

One of my students recently asked me if I still have doubts about my healing work or my connection to spirit, and I must admit, it really made me think. I had a long delay before answering, not because I didn't know, but because I began to think of all the questions I'd had answered during my spiritual journey to this point. I suppose there will always be questions that pop up, and in fact in anyone's mind who starts to develop spiritual practices, after all, we are dealing with much that is unseen and requires our complete trust.

I believe that it is important to ask questions when you get the opportunity. I know that in the early part of my training I asked anyone I considered to be more experienced than me various questions about how they were taught, and about their beliefs and experiences etc. I believe that our mind wants to be fed information when we are searching and especially when we are uncertain in ourselves. I also believe that those who have had proof and have practical experience are much more confident and trusting in the spiritual ways and therefor, question less because they have practical experience and many results to work with.

I thought for the purpose of this book and especially for the new students of spiritual healing that it would be good to share some of the questions I have asked and had answered by spiritual healers and some, which have been put to me by my own students over the course of time. I will start with what I believe to be the simplest and probably most common and work forward. I must admit, when I look back at some of the first questions I asked and the things I didn't know back then, it lets me see how far I've come. I really hope these questions help you to grow in the same way.

Q – Can anybody have the gift of healing?

A – Everyone has the ability within themselves to heal; this is how we recover from illness but those who are naturally compassionate often have an ability to heal others and when they choose to share that with others, it then becomes a gift.

Q – Is Spiritual Healing different from other healing?
A – People who are natural healers are born with compassion which can be transformed into a healing energy, and that comes from the person. The spiritual healer builds a connection with the spirit and learns to become a channel for the love and compassion of the spiritual energy. There are other methods of healing which I will bring in as we go on.

Q – Do I need to have faith or belief in healing for it to work?
A – I have seen healing work very powerfully on those who know and even believe it will help them, but equally, I have seen many times, people who have no belief or faith being healed and they also recover. I often point people to cases where animals or even babies who have no knowledge that they are being given healing energy and yet thrive on it and get over what has caused them illness.

I think that things like faith and belief do help but aren't really necessary.

Q – Is it more important if the healer feels heat in their hands when they are giving healing to people?
A – I know lots of healers who experience the sense of heat building in their hands when they pass healing to someone, but there are others whose hands turn cold, and even some who sense no change of temperature. In my experience, I have had all three descriptions occur and I put it down to my spirit guide, who I believe channels the correct energy for the individual and sometimes it is hot, cold or neither. Actually, I've even had all three in one healing. I believe that the change in temperature happens a lot in the beginning and it helps the new healer to understand that something different is happening. Over the course of my work, I now just trust and go with the flow, as I am sure the spirit will do the right thing.

Q – Sometimes when I practice my healing on people, I feel their pain, is this right?

A - There are healers who do mirror the pain of their patient; it's like a sympathetic pain that lets the healer truly empathise with the condition they are working on. I believe that with some patients we connect at different levels and that it doesn't always happen, and it is stronger with some more than others. Just remember, the pain is not yours and it will leave, it is only an emotional reflection of your patients suffering, it won't really affect you.

Q – Do I need to touch my patients before I work on them?

A – Healers don't have to touch their patients to pass healing energy to them. There are healers who like to start by gently placing their hands on the persons shoulder or holding hands before lifting them up and working in the aura around them. If you work like this it is always better to get the person's permission to lay your hands on them before you begin. I believe that healers should always inform their patients or clients of the practice before they begin and always make sure that the person is fully aware of your process before you continue. In cases of healers who work by the laying on of hands, once again I would just say that you should get the person's permission before you begin.

Q – How long should my healing practice last for?
A – Healing sessions do not have to be long to have a good effect. I find that my sessions run for approximately fifteen minutes when I begin. I also talk to my patient before I begin and then ask them how they are feeling at the end, so around about half an hour all together. But some healings are longer depending on the person's need etc. As a spiritual healer I tend to allow the spirit to look after the timing and they always get it just right.

Q - Do I have to meditate for a long time before each healing I give, and do I have to meditate at the end to rebuild my energy?
A – Every healer is different and will find what is right for them. The spiritual development that I did and still do means that I prepare my mind in my circle each week and link to the spirit who balance my energy and prepare it for

all the work I have in the coming week. This means I can take just a short moment to clear my mind to practice my healing. I tend to feel good after my healing sessions because I have been in the spiritual power when I'm channelling, so if anything, I get a boost from my work. I would just say to any healers who do feel drained after healing that it is sometimes better to ground yourself in the physical world as it helps bring mind and body together quicker than mental exercise such as meditation. Just do normal things.

Q – Why isn't there just one type of healing? I hear of so many different practices like "Reiki and crystal healing and even quantum healing, how is it different?
A – I believe that true healing is the same no matter what people call it or what they use to cause it. I have also learned that people are very different in how they accept things such as healing, and therefore I would dare to say it's people who are different and not healing. If it comes from any healer who is compassionate and has good intentions, it will be healing by any name. I feel in my

heart that people who are drawn to the practices of healing should study and practice what they feel sits right with them.

Q – Is prayer a source of healing? Does it matter who you pray to?
A – In simple terms I would say, yes. Praying for the betterment of another person or even situation to get better is an act of compassion and therefore is a form of healing. I say this to those who pray from their heart and not for selfish reasons. I direct my prayers to my spirit guide because this works for me. If you direct your prayers to The God of your religion, or even Goddesses, etc, I believe the higher power is all one, and it is us who need to have an individual need for one over the other. When it comes to wanting to help, I would say that comes from the good in us and any form of higher power would encourage that.

Q What is distant healing and how does it work?
A – Distant or Absent healing, is like a concentrated prayer combined with an out of body experience. Certain healers

can mentally be present with a patient who is a distance away from them and can still affect a healing with the mind. For me it happens a bit like that, only I feel my guide has travelled with me and is channelling through my mind and light-body. When you become more accustomed to letting go in your meditation practice, it is easier to understand how your light-body can work separately from the physical, but until you get to that point, simply pray and ask your guides to help you send healing energy to those you wish to share with.

Q – If our circle work together with distant healing, is it stronger?
A – when I have been part of a circle and we have linked together to send healing en-masse, it really does seem to be more powerful and the recipient in such cases have genuinely felt that the energy really helps them.

Q – Is it okay to send healing to the dying even if they are going to pass anyway?
A – It is absolutely okay to send to people in the last moments of their life as the act and energy of healing in

such times can have an effect on both the dying person, as it helps them to move easily into the spirit world, and for their loved ones, it can also help with the grief which will following the passing. I and many other healers work with those who are in preparation for their passing, as the spirit have taught that death is not the opposite of life, it is actually a part of it.

Q – Is there ever a time when we shouldn't do or send healing to someone?
A – I have learned that there is a time to heal and a time when we must leave it alone. The practicing healer can feel in their heart when they must open and channel their gift, and equally, they can feel when it is time to stand back and learn from the act of not healing. Like all spiritual gifts, healing is a soul energy, and the soul speaks to us all when we listen. I learned more about this kind of thing the longer I sat in my development circle and bonded with my guide.

Q – Can we turn healing gifts on and off?

A As a spiritual healer I would always say that it is our choice to heal or not. The spirit that works through me will be present when I open to use my gift, and they will know when it is right to do so, but if I choose not to, that would be my choice and spirit will respect this. I believe that all healers and mediums etc, should find a balance in their life that allows them to share their gifts with others but equally have time for a personal life too. Being a healer teaches you all about balance.

Q – Is it selfish to use your healing gift on yourself?
A – I believe that it is essential to always see yourself as a sentient human being, that could benefit from healing as much as anyone else. I encourage all my students to practice healing on themselves, mind, body and spirit. I must say that I learned a lot practicing healing on myself and my life.

Q – Why do the spirits need healers to channel when they could just pass healing to anyone and why don't they?

A – The spirit does not need healers but when a healer awakes in this world it is because they have become aware of the suffering of others and compassion is born in them, it is this moment when the spirit guide begins to bond with them. It is the act of healing from one person to another that can encourage more compassion and empathy between people and that is a very good thing. The action of healing between people shows that there is a power greater than self achievement or individual needs.

There is more to Spiritual Healing than just trying to make people better. The act of healing is a spiritual one and has far reaching consequences, in a good way. Also, the spirit does heal without a human healer, but there are many things in a human life that must be felt, experienced and understood, and often the natural law of the Universe does not allow for this. A good thing to take from this, is when more healers and spiritual practitioners are in our world there will be more love and caring for each other.

Q – How will I know bad teacher from a good one, and how will I know they are right for me?

A - Many people have to go through different teachers to find the right one as I did. Looking back, I can see that I was guided to mine, but had to learn lessons on the way. I would say that you should check out local Spiritualist Churches, or healing centres in your area. People in these places will know who has a good reputation because of word of mouth. I would also say be careful of adverts in magazines and such, as you might want to get some real feedback on a spiritual teacher before committing to them. A true teacher will make you feel at ease and balanced, not excited or overwhelmed, so watch for this.

Q- Do you enjoy being a healer?

A – I have loved my healing practice and everything I have learned from using it. To say that I have truly found my purpose would be an understatement. Being a healer has allowed me to know a side of myself that needed to grow and open and experience things about people in this world that I might never have got to know had I not followed this path. In short, I would have to say that I love being a healer because it has changed my life and allowed me to help and assist many others.

I really hope that the question and answers I have shared with you are helpful and that they might inspire you to dig deeper into the subject and learn even more about the wonderful gift of Spiritual Healing. In sharing this with you it has brought up one big question in me that I would like to ask you and that is.

**"If you have the sense that you have the gift of healing within you, when are you going to share it?"**

Printed in Great Britain
by Amazon